LONE
TREE

ALSO BY BRUCE BROWN

Mountain in the Clouds

LONE TREE

A True Story of Murder
in America's Heartland

BRUCE BROWN

CROWN PUBLISHERS INC.
NEW YORK

For my parents,
Malcolm and Marian Brown

Published by Crown Publishers, Inc., 201 East 50th Street,
New York, New York 10022.

CROWN is a trademark of Crown Publishers, Inc.

Manufactured in the United States of America

Library of Congress Cataloging-in-Publication Data

Brown, Bruce.
    Lone tree / by Bruce Brown.
        p.   cm.
    I. Title.
PS3552.R68524L66   1988
813'.54—dc19   88-38058
                                                          CIP

ISBN 0-517-56987-6

Book design by Kingsley Parker

10 9 8 7 6 5 4 3 2 1

First Edition

PART ONE

Praise big farms, stick to little ones.
                                        Virgil

1

The sound of gunfire was frequently heard on the Dale Burr farm. Every fall for decades, shotguns crackled in ragged bursts through the early-morning hours, becoming as much a part of the local scene as the hog calls that farmers used to summon their animals in the days before self-feeders.

Old-timers say that when they were young, the best pheasant hunting in Johnson County, Iowa, was out near the town of Lone Tree, on the Dale Burr place. Every year in early winter people drove from as far away as Hills, Iowa City, and even Muscatine in the next county to try their luck in Dale Burr's corn.

Some of these sportsmen hunted in off the county spur road to the east, without knowledge of or permission from the man whose fields they walked. Most, however, came to the back door of the Burrs' large white farmhouse first. With shotguns cradled casually in their arms, they would ask if they could hunt the 160 acres behind.

It is customary for hunters to leave the farmer a share of the pheasants they take from his land, and so the Burrs ate a lot of pheasants they did not kill. Actually, birding privileges on the Burrs' place were prized enough that some people would ply Dale with gifts for months before, like the cantaloupes a group of melon farmers down by Coneville brought over every summer.

If Dale was in the house, he would come out and have a few words with the men standing in a half-circle around the back porch. More often, though, the hunters found him working around the hog houses or one of his two barns. A tall man with a hearty laugh and handskake, he let just about everybody he knew hunt the place in those days, and would even suggest where the birds might be at that time of day and year. He'd say they might walk the northeast 40, or perhaps try down through the adjoining pasture and hay fields. Good friends were invited to stay for dinner or at least coffee and some of his wife Emily's pie on their way out, and all received his wish of good luck.

Many of those who loaded their guns and fanned out across his fields must have privately wished for a little of Dale Burr's luck, for his farm was in every respect a fine one. The eye was first attracted to the classic two-story frame farmhouse set back in the trees, the dark bulk of the barns, stables, farrowing houses, and assorted outbuildings, the prize-winning cattle and sheep, the well-tended equipment. But those who went out and got their boots muddy could see that the land itself was the best part of the Dale Burr place. A portion of that great swath of silty loam that undulates across southwest Iowa, Lincoln Township land like Dale Burr's is among the nation's most productive.

One hundred fifty years ago, this land nourished the tall grass prairie, that shimmering sea of bluestem reaching so high it could hide a horse and rider. Lone Tree, Iowa, the nearest town, located a couple miles south of the Burrs on the county blacktop, takes its name from a giant elm that was once the only tree on the trail between the Mississippi and Iowa rivers. In those days, the Sac and Fox Indians claimed this land, and Totokonock, the prophet who predicted victory for Black Hawk in the ill-fated war that bears the great chief's name, lived nearby. Part of Dale Burr's farm was included in the so-called Black Hawk Purchase of 1832, which took the land from the Indians after Black Hawk's defeat at the Battle of the Bad Axe.

As the virgin prairie was laboriously turned under, Iowa pioneers discovered that the soil beneath was rich beyond their wildest expectations. Many exotic crops—including Pacific salmon from California—were planted by nineteenth-century Iowa pioneers, but in the long run the most reliable crops proved to be ones that resembled important portions of the vanishing prairie. Corn, or Indian maize, which is itself a giant member of the grass family, replaced the bluestem as the dominant ground cover. Similarly, the American bison was superseded by domestic cattle, and the prairie chicken, which was once the reigning fowl of the region, was replaced by an unrelated but similar gallinaceous bird from the plains of Asia, the China pheasant.

First introduced to North America in the nineteenth century, these dramatic coppery birds with elegant red and green accents took to the country quickly. The classic Midwestern mixture of pasture and grain gave them the grassy nesting areas they need for summer reproduction, as well as winter cover and a rich and abundant supply of food. Because of their beauty, size, and excellent eating, pheasants quickly developed a fervent following among Midwestern hunters, who take them any way possible.

Kids will drive old pickups out into the fields in dry weather to pursue the birds at high speed down the corn stubble rows. And during freezing rainstorms, some farmers have been known to go ice skating down gravel roads with clubs to harvest pheasants huddling helpless and temporarily blinded in roadside ditches.

Pheasant hunting on the Dale Burr place during the late 1950s and early 1960s was more refined than this, though. It was the classic Midwestern pheasant quest, with the men and boys walking alone, or strung out in a loose line. Their weapons were shotguns, mostly 12-gauge, with an occasional lighter 16- or 20-gauge, and most were pumps. Dogs sometimes assisted in flushing and retrieving birds, but there was no getting drunk and spraying mud around. Some of the people who carried guns across Dale's fields did not really seem to care if they got a bird or not. Dale Burr's was a place you could go to simply appreciate the aching beauty of the landscape as winter tightened its grip.

Hunting there was honest sport too, since the birds could easily elude their pursuers, especially in the shadowy, whispering world of the ripe standing corn. Like outrageously plumed chickens, the pheasants strutted up and down the rows playing peek-a-boo with the hunters. It was a rare marksman who could bag a pheasant in the corn, even if he saw it first, for the birds simply were too fast. In fact, the only way to hunt pheasants with some degree of certainty is to drive them from cover in front of a hunter who is at the ready, with his gun up and a round in the chamber. Even then, if the angle of the birds' rise into the air or its shearing descent to the next field is off even a little, the hunter will miss.

Dale Burr himself had hunted pheasant since he was a teenager, but in those days there were no birds to speak of in Johnson County, or anywhere else in southeast Iowa. During the late 1930s, Dale and his father, Vernon, did much of their hunting in northeast Iowa. It was here, near the town of Winthrop, that the Burr clan went pheasant hunting the morning after the famous Armistice Day 1940 storm. Seventeen men died along the Mississippi as an early blizzard swept in on the night of November 10. Most were duck hunters who had gone out to spend the night in blinds along the river. The survivors burned cedar duck decoys, many of them quite expensive, to stay warm until morning.

Bob Berry, a cousin of Dale's, remembers the world seemed new-made that morning. He, Dale, Vernon, and several other cousins found the sloughs along the Mississippi thick with ducks, which circled continuously in the steaming water. The men were almost distracted from their aim for pheasant when they found the Chinas thick too. The sudden deep snow made the birds uncommonly easy to track. One bird flushed nearby, and then flew directly over them. They all had a good shot at the bird, but it flew on, apparently unscathed. The Burrs were just marveling out loud at the bird's amazing flight when it suddenly plummeted straight down dead. Others were easier. The six men in the party all got their three-bird limit by mid-morning, for a total of eighteen birds killed in the space of a few hours.

What Dale Burr liked about pheasant hunting was the fellowship, the break from the work of the farm, and the edge of excitement in seeing what fortune might bring. Guns were not a big thing with him, nor was killing, although he was a good shot and liked bringing home game. As much as anything, he just enjoyed having the birds around, and so after World War II he gladly assisted a neighborhood effort to establish pheasants around Lone Tree. The first step came when a neighbor, Eugene Weise, raised some pheasant chicks and released them on his place to the north. That winter Dale left a good-size patch of corn standing to carry the birds through until spring. Within a few years, the pheasant population had mushroomed. Dale's son, John, recalls that when he started hunting in the late 1950s it was not unusual to startle up two hundred pheasants at once from behind a haystack on the Burr place.

National farm policy at the time also contributed to the increase in southeast Iowa pheasants, albeit inadvertently. During the Eisenhower Administration, then-record farm surpluses prompted Congress to create a raft of federal programs designed to increase conservation and decrease production. Primary among these was the Soil Bank (which paid Iowa farmers $54 million to fallow more than one million acres in 1956, the first year of the program's existence), but the government was also aiding and abetting the birds in many smaller, less obvious, and less expensive ways. One that Johnson County farmers took advantage of was the program that gave rosebushes to farmers who wanted to hedgerow their fence lines. The idea was to create windbreaks for soil conservation, but in the process pheasants received excellent year-round cover.

The reason the birds especially favored the Burr place was the corn. Dale Burr routinely had the last standing corn for forty miles around. Pheasants gathered here for food and shelter when the blizzards howled. While many farmers, especially the more devoted hunters, might appreciate this, very few would do it themselves because leaving corn in the field meant forgoing income from land they would have already invested money in plowing, seeding, cultivating, and fertilizing. And so by late November every year,

Dale Burr generally was the only big farmer in the vicinity with unharvested corn. "This gave him what you might call his own hunting preserve," recounted a friend, who added that a favorite neighborhood hunting tactic was to "chase the birds out of Dale's corn into the surrounding fields, and shoot them there."

In those days, Dale mostly hunted with Bob Berry, Keith Forbes, Vernon Burr, and other relatives. Even in old age, Dale's father, Vernon, was avid enough about pheasants to carry a shotgun with him on the tractor so as not to miss a shot at a prize cock. Then, on the weekends, most of the men in the Burr family would go pheasant hunting in earnest. Keith Forbes recalls that "Dale probably went less than some of us, but that wasn't because he wasn't a good hunter or didn't enjoy hunting. He just worked more Saturdays. So I guess you'd say it was a little special when he came along. We'd generally get going in mid-morning after chores, and always have our limit by noon. Afterward, we'd all get together at Dale's place for one of Emily's dinners."

Although no one else in the family left corn standing through the winter, Dale's practice was very much what people in Johnson County call "a Burr thing to do." Without having come from a family that has spent several generations in this Iowa community, as the Burrs have, it is probably impossible to fully savor the meaning of this expression, but generally it refers to a quiet, underlying sense of values evident in the family's tendency to do the right thing as they saw it, even if it cost money. Vernon and his wife, Hilda, were strict Presbyterians and expected a lot of their kids, Dale and Ruth. "Understand," another old friend said of the family, "these were very moral people."

A cousin recalled that when he and Dale were around ten years old, their favorite game was to trap English sparrows in one of the hog sheds by closing the door behind them once the sparrows had flown inside. Then, seizing corncobs from the floor, they would attempt to hit the birds in flight. More than once, their errant pegs were punctuated by the tinkle of falling windowpanes, which they hoped Vernon would not notice. He did notice, of course, but he was not the one who eventually put an end to the game. One summer day, Dale stopped his cousins from killing a desperate bird with the comment that startled them so much that one remembered it over a half-century later. "God," young Dale admonished his friends sternly, "sees every sparrow that falls."

A few years later at the Johnson County Fair in Iowa City, some "city toughs" were harassing the country boys by throwing handfuls of straw off the floor into the buckets of water they were carrying to their livestock. Rather than feed their pampered animals dirty water, farm boy after farm boy turned aside, threw his water away, and went back for more. The pattern was repeated with increasing mirth among the perpetrators until one of them threw a handful of filth in the bucket of water Dale Burr was carrying to his calf. Dale looked at the water for an instant, as if entranced, and then threw it all over the snickering city slick. Howling with rage, the older boy came at Dale in a flash, but the other farm boys rallied to Dale's defense, and the troublemakers were forced to take a soggy walk.

Members of the Burr family recall this incident as a rarity. They always said Dale took after his uncle George Nelson. Hilda's brother was famous around Lone Tree for his calm disposition. Once when a bearing went out on his tractor (an expensive, time-consuming breakdown), he was heard to exclaim, "Oh, fiddle, it just doesn't give a fellow a chance." Ruth Forbes said of her brother, Dale, "He was a very calm sort of person, and not one to speak his opinions openly." Again and again, in the face of the countless difficulties that are endemic to farming, Dale Burr showed uncommon equanimity. He was never known to raise his voice in anger at anyone, and there were more than a few times when his warm laughter cheered a relative or neighbor.

Yet others heard what they took to be the ring of arrogance in his laughter. One time a fellow came out and offered Dale Burr $10,000 for a mare he had raised. Dale leaned forward on the corral. "If that horse is worth ten thousand to you," he said with a chuckle, "she's worth twice that to me." An old horse associate characterized this quip as "typical Dale." So too was the eventual outcome, for Dale did, in fact, refuse to sell the horse. It seemed sometimes as if the Burrs not only followed their own law; they were above those that applied to everyone else. While most Johnson County farmers were early risers, the Burrs worked late into the night. Similarly, since farming knows no eight-hour days or weekends, a neighbor was struck when Dale told him once that he would die before he'd work on Sunday.

Although he stood an honest six feet tall, people remember Dale Burr as a larger man. This was probably due to his solid presence and the obvious power of his well-muscled physique, especially his hands. Farmers' hands are often like books, and Dale's were two volumes of Tolstoy. Large, broad, and deeply weathered, they were equally capable of cinching down a flailing animal or performing minute adjustments on sophisticated machinery. His eyes were blue, and his features clean and boyish. Work had stiffened his movements somewhat over the years, but his carriage remained upright. In fact, the most obvious mark of age on Dale was the disappearance of his wavy black head of hair. Otherwise, his features were still those of the boy staring out of a snapshot taken more than a half-century ago.

This picture shows Dale sitting in a field with a group of chums. The bill of his baseball cap is turned up like an "Our Gang" character's, and he is grinning the unrestrained, perfect-toothed smile of a boy who has just spent a few cherished hours playing baseball. It isn't hard to see why Dale Burr was named the "Healthiest Boy" in Johnson County after a school sports meet. He played baseball, basketball, and football at Lone Tree High School during the Depression, and was elected president of his class senior year. The thing that people remember most about Dale, though, was his ability to work. Even in a community where grueling physical labor was common coinage, Dale Burr stood out. His father, Vernon, used to say, "My son has carried more corn on his shoulders than any man in Iowa."

As a young man, he married Emily Wacker, daughter of a prominent banker in the neighboring town of Wilton. Vernon Burr gave the couple a 160-acre farm with a fine white farmhouse, and Emily filled it with truckloads of antiques from her family's big house in Wilton. In time she bore three talented children whom Dale loved deeply and openly. The kind of father who not only encouraged his kids in worthwhile activity but actually took the lead in making it possible, Dale Burr was the driving force behind the formation of the 4-H chapter called the Prairie Masters.

A low-keyed but rock-ribbed Republican and longtime Farm Bureau member, Dale expanded until the 160 acres his father originally staked him to had swelled to more than

500 acres, not including the 200-plus acres owned by his son, John, and his mother, Hilda, which were farmed in a loose unit with his own holdings. Taken together with his close cousins among the Burrs, Stocks, Berrys, and Mussers, Dale's family controlled thousands of acres of Johnson County farmland.

Although he favored unpretentious work clothes and rarely bought a new car, Dale himself was one of the wealthiest farmers around Lone Tree. In December 1983, the Hills Bank and Trust Company, one of the three area banks with which he did business, estimated Dale Burr's worth at $1.76 million.

One of the few things anyone heard Dale complain about then was the pheasants. Ever since the 1970s, the birds had been in decline. To get an idea of how much things had changed, John Burr said that when he was a teenager they used to kill a half-dozen nesting hen pheasants mowing a twenty-acre hay field. In 1984, the Burrs' mowers did not hit any.

Dale became more and more restrictive about whom he would allow to hunt, and finally closed the place to hunting altogether. He still left the corn standing in the field late, and refused to fall plow. In addition, he invested thousands of dollars in erosion-control projects such as check dams and contouring. Still the number of birds dwindled. Because the pheasant families wandered about without respect to property lines, it was impossible to separate Dale's place from its neighbors. They were all bound together.

Like the prior Johnson County pheasant boom, the birds' disappearance was due to many factors, most of them related to agricultural practices and national farm policy. Farmers were using more pesticides and herbicides, planting more of their land in row crops, and removing trees and windbreaks. All were symptoms of large-scale industrial agriculture pushing the land for maximum production (regardless of the immediate cost in dollars or the ultimate loss of soil), and all were then being encouraged by the government. In Johnson County, Iowa, farmers were even subsidized to remove the rosebushes they had been given to plant two decades before.

Unlike his Republican predecessor, President Richard Nixon was not interested in limiting food production. He saw agricultural surpluses as a tool of American diplomacy and a weapon in realpolitik. Consequently, conservation programs were downplayed. In one of his better-known pronouncements, Nixon's secretary of agriculture, Earl Butz, urged farmers to plant "from fencerow to fencerow." Butz also pushed large-scale farming, which he saw as more cost-efficient and scientific. Spurred by this overt pressure from Washington, as well as a host of covert encouragements (such as the fact that virtually all federal agricultural research is directed toward the problems of large agribusiness-type operations), many of Iowa's best, forward-looking young farmers went deeply into debt to buy larger spreads and more equipment.

With their land as collateral, they borrowed large amounts of money, sometimes more than their farming fathers had made in a lifetime, and reinvested it in farming. The 1970s saw a tremendous modernizing, upgrading, and expanding of America's agricultural plant. The Burr farm was only one of many that collected an impressive array of shiny new farm machinery. By the late 1970s, land sales began to develop a feeding-frenzy quality. Amid popular drum beating on the dangers of overpopulation and famine, the price of good Johnson County farmland soared from $1,200 to

$2,200 to $3,200 an acre, with no apparent end in sight. Americans began to think with pride of agriculture as the nation's "answer to OPEC," and many urbanites were pleased to learn that the United States was still the world's largest exporter of virtually every basic food, from corn to wheat to soybeans to rice.

Then, in 1980, President Jimmy Carter imposed an embargo on American grain sales to the Soviet Union in retaliation for the invasion of Afghanistan. While Nixon had intoned on the power of agricultural diplomacy, Carter learned that there was also great vulnerability in America's highly leveraged, export-dependent agriculture, for his Soviet embargo marked the beginning of a world trend away from American agricultural produce. Not only did the Soviets find other more congenial suppliers, but many American allies did likewise as world food production increased in every hemisphere. Farmers reacted with rage toward Carter, but his successor only made things worse. Under President Ronald Reagan, American's domination of world agriculture eroded further, and the chronic American agricultural distress erupted into a full-blown agricultural crisis.

With most basic food crops being produced at or near new records (American farmers grew an all-time high 2.1 billion bushels of wheat in 1982, for instance) and export markets drying up, the government began to acquire surpluses, which themselves soon reached record highs. Commodity prices fell, land values fell, loans were called or could not be met when they came due, and thousands of acres were foreclosed. Hardest hit of all were the nation's family farmers, for whom Iowa is a stronghold. By the winter of 1984, an estimated one in three were in financial trouble. The chill reality of foreclosure was as close for them as the snow on the window ledge, and it cast a pall that was particularly apparent during the holidays.

By comparison, Christmas 1984 seemed a typically festive occasion in the Dale Burr household. Emily made her famous holiday candy and cookies, including the fudge that was a favorite of Dale and John's. "She'd start baking it in late November to get a head start on the season," recalled John. "Dad and I would get into it and eat as much as half the batch. When she caught us, we'd say, 'This was good, but not quite perfect. Maybe we could make some more.' Yeah, Dad and I had that one worked out pretty well," he laughed. Just before Christmas, the Burrs' two grown daughters, Sheila and Julia, came home from out of state.

It was traditional in the Dale Burr household to open presents on Christmas morning, but actually the process went on for weeks. In a title transfer registered December 24, 1984, for instance, Dale and Emily gave John a fractional interest in the home place worth thousands of dollars "in consideration of the sum of one dollar, Love and Affection." John Burr also received more than $30,000 cash from his father in December and January.

Although they suggested prosperity, these gifts were really a sign that things were not entirely right at the Burrs'. Even if one knew this, though, who would have suspected that Christmas 1984 would be Emily and Dale Burr's last, or that the next time Dale picked up his shotgun it would be to hunt people he knew and loved well?

Who would have thought that in less than a year, Dale Burr would directly affect American agricultural policy, be discussed from Singapore to Schenectady, and ultimately trace the mark of agricultural history since the reign of Henry VIII in the good Iowa dirt?

2

Before December 9, 1985, the best-known landmark around Lone Tree, Iowa, was probably the neon sign at the intersection of highways 22 and X-14 on the outskirts of town. Over a dozen feet high and shaped like a stylized Grant Wood tree, it proclaimed the name Lone Tree in two-foot-high red letters.

The sign had originally been part of the Lone Tree Motel in Des Moines, but when that estimable establishment was forced to close, the owner contacted the town of Lone Tree to see if it wanted to acquire the sign. The answer was yes, and so the neon tree was trucked more than one hundred miles from the state capital to its new home out past the Lone Tree Cemetery.

It was about this time that the original lone tree—the one that gave the town its name—died. Located out on the southeast side of town in an old farmyard, it succumbed to disease and was cut down. A few old-timers felt a pang at its passing, but most people in town were not aware of any great loss. As if to belie its name, almost every street in Lone Tree had been planted with gracious shade trees. By the 1970s, Lone Tree might have been more accurately called Many Trees.

Some of the nicest specimens are in the town park, around the tennis courts, horseshoe pits, commodious barbecue facilities, and the World War II vintage tank that aims its spiked gun across the street at the American Legion hall. Centrally located between the park and the cemetery, the American Legion provides the social nexus of the community in many ways. In fact, it says much about Lone Tree that the largest, most impressive building in town does not belong to the bank or the implement dealer. It belongs to the American Legion post.

Endowed with a sizable bequest from a farmer who had no heirs, the Legion is in a position to set standards in the community. More than a few people commented, for instance, when the Legion paved its entire parking lot and entry drive, covering a couple of acres with concrete. The Legion contributes generously to local causes and charities every year, and its modern building—which boasts a dramatic central skylight—is in heavy demand from people as far away as Hills for all manner of community affairs and activities.

It was here in the Lone Tree American Legion that Dale Burr made a speech that many people around town still remember. The occasion was Dale's forty-year high-school class reunion in 1981. Without any warning that his friends and relatives saw, Dale stood up and gave a speech about what farming meant to him. There was a lot of talk and laughter in the room when Dale began, but it quickly subsided as the middle-aged former football stars and cheerleaders tugged on each others' sleeves and gestured with their drinks.

What got their attention was not so much Dale's actual words, but the realization that what he was saying was an expression of the heart, and an unusual insight into a man whom they had known all their lives, but few could say they really knew. Dale talked of the generations of Burrs who had farmed around Lone Tree, and of his own love of the land. At the end, when he had all of their attention, he said he "hoped to die with my boots on," which made the audience laugh, since they assumed he meant his famous manure-covered barn boots.

At the same time, the class of 1941 reunion crowd was touched by the personal nature of Dale's statement. They knew he was not exaggerating his family's deep ties to the land. His father was a farmer, as was his father before him, and his father before him. In fact, the Burrs had been farmers as far back as the family could trace its ancestors—before they ever saw Iowa, or even America. Although their specific identities have been lost, it appears that the Burrs were descended from English or lowland Scots yeomen whose history offers a revealing parallel to the more recent experience of the Burrs in America.

Freer than the common European serf, the yeomen were known as particularly diligent and dependable workers, qualities that modern dictionaries still associate with the word. Contemporaries recognized the yeoman as a special characteristic of English culture, as well as a source of the national strength. One reflection of this can be seen in William Langland's fourteenth-century allegorical poem "The Vision of Piers the Plowman," where the yeoman is identified with the highest forms of human attainment. Another, more prosaic, indication of the yeoman's importance to

England emerged in the Hundred Years' War. The rough longbow archers who slaughtered the flower of French chivalry at Crécy in 1346 were yeomen all.

The cornerstone of the yeoman economy was the commons, that great body of public land that was traditionally available during the Middle Ages to the various classes of yeoman: the bond holder, the script holder, and the tenant. Much of the commons was forested (indeed, the yeoman in Chaucer's *Canterbury Tales* was a forester), but a goodly portion of it was also grazed as common pasture or tilled in the common field system of small holdings packed together in winding wormlike slips along the river bottoms. Neither the milk he got from his cow, nor the salmon he netted in the river, nor the wood he gathered from the forest, nor the part-time wages he earned laboring for the lord were enough to sustain the yeoman alone, but through their combination he fashioned a life for himself and his family.

The destruction of this economy, and with it the free yeomanry, began in the mid-thirteenth century with the passage of the first English statutes sanctioning enclosure. The term *enclosure* referred to large private landowners' enclosing what had been public commons with fences, ditches, and hedges. The intent of the original statutes seems to have been to promote the reclamation of wasteland, but with the rise of the Flemish wool trade, the laws were made to serve another purpose. After the fourteenth century, the lords of England used enclosure extensively to evict yeomen from their traditional homes and transform common fields to sheep pasture.

Saint Thomas More was referring to the enclosures when he observed in *Utopia,* "Your shepe that were wont to be so meke and tame, and so small eaters, now . . . become so great devourers and so wylde that they eat up, and swallow down the very men themselves." The prospects for yeomen who lost their fields or homes to the wool industry were not good, for as More observed: "The husbandman be thrust owte of their owne, or else either by coveyne and fraude, or by violent oppression are put beside it. . . . And when they have wandered abrode tyll that be spent, and can they else do but steale and then justly pardy be hanged, or else go about begging."

The king of England hardly saw this as cause for grieving, though. In 1535, shortly after he had Thomas More executed, Henry VIII ordered monasteries in England to stop providing charity to the dispossessed yeomen, thereby cutting off their main source of relief. As a result, English yeomen by the thousands were driven out of the country into the burgeoning cities. There they slaved in the wool trade for the profit of the very enterprises that played so large a part in evicting them. In the process, they also helped fill the tax coffers of the English crown. Like many since, the Tudor "prosperity" was fueled by a vast transfer of wealth from the many to the few.

All across England, the number of small farms declined steadily as the average size of the surviving farms increased. The rural population declined steadily too, but agricultural production actually increased, thanks to the growing use after 1688 of more sophisticated Dutch agricultural techniques that eliminated the fallow year in the traditional crop rotation, and utilized roots as winter livestock feed. The ability to carry more livestock through the winter soon enabled the English farmer to dramatically improve the breeding of his animals. At the same time, farm machinery, like Jethro Tull's revolutionary seed drill, came into use for the first time, making it possible for one man to do the work of many.

As food prices rose, the direction of the enclosures reversed so that most of the land was being converted from pasture to food crops. The concentration of farm ownership continued to increase, however, as did the size of farms. By the eighteenth century, farms under one hundred acres were dwindling, while those over three hundred acres were multiplying. Nearly 3,500 separate bills of enclosure were passed by Parliament between 1717 and 1820, and between 1740 and 1788 alone the number of farms declined by forty thousand. Many refused to leave the homes of their forefathers, and so it was increasingly necessary to pull down the houses of the evicted, as is described at the outset of Thomas Hardy's *The Mayor of Casterbridge*.

The English ruling class dismissed the resulting distress as inconsequential, and loudly applauded the process that increased its own power as social progress. Jeremy Bentham, the father of Utilitarianism, thought the spectacle of enclosure one of the most reassuring evidences of happiness and advancement to be seen in the realm. Much talk of improving the morals of the poor can be found in the lordly discussion of enclosures during the early nineteenth century, but the driving motive remained baldly economic. Large English interests not only benefited directly from the initial enclosure and addition to their lands, but they also profited from the resulting drop in wages and increased demand for manufactured goods of all types.

Needless to say, the majority of the yeomen viewed things much differently than those who sat on soft chairs in London or Manchester. For them, the enclosures were a mortal threat and a moral outrage. They saw ancient customs being shattered to strip them of the richest portion of their livelihood, and force them to fall back on wage labor as the sole means of support at a time when wages were falling and prices rising. Yeoman resistance was evident for five hundred years, with particularly virulent outbreaks occurring in the Peasants' Revolt of 1381 and Ket's Insurrection of 1549.

In Germany, where small farmers struggled against a more rigidly feudal aristocracy, the rising wave of insurrections culminated in the Great Peasant War. Repeatedly rebuffed in their effort to win recognition of simple freedoms —including restoration of enclosed lands—the peasants went to war in 1524. Their armies commanded much of Franconia, Swabia, and Thuringia, but the aristocratic forces were much better equipped. After Martin Luther condemned the insurrection in *Against the Murderous and Thieving Peasant Hordes,* these forces inflicted terrible retribution on the peasants. An estimated 100,000 peasants were killed, and those who remained lost all political rights.

In England, the issue was not finally resolved until 1830, when a killing sheep epidemic struck England, and thousands of Englishmen were forced to subsist on sorrel and roots. In many cases, the farm laborer née yeoman was worse fed and clothed than prisoners in the jail. Finally, anger over "The Thing," as *Political Register* editor William Cobbett called the conspiracy of the rich against the poor, sparked the Kent Uprising of August 1830. It began when threshing machines were put into operation in that part of southeast England for the first time, thus eliminating one of the last remaining rural hand industries that paid decently.

The insurrection exploded across most of southern and eastern England in the glow of midnight arson, but once again, hungry, ill-equipped farmers proved no match for professional soldiers. By winter, the rebellion had been brutally suppressed. It was clear that neither the enclosures nor the power that wielded them could be resisted. "The small farmer either emigrated to America or to an industrial town, or became a day laborer," observed J. L. and Barbara Hammond in their classic study of the later enclosures, *The Village Labourer, 1760–1832.* Dale Burr's great-great-grandfather was apparently one of these, for the Burrs materialized in Massachusetts a short time later.

Nelson Burr, Dale's great-grandfather, lived near the town of Lenox, Massachusetts, during the 1840s with his wife, Lydia Percival, and their infant son, Levi. A born and bred farmer, Nelson soon grew frustrated with western Massachusetts. The area was rocky, and had an air of the old country in both its names and history. Great Barrington, barely a dozen miles down the Housatonic Valley from Lenox, was the site of an infamous debtors jail that helped spur Shays's Rebellion. A half-century had passed since Daniel Shays was defeated, but there was still a trace of the residual bitterness that remains wherever government troops have been used to enforce bankers' mortgages on small farmers.

Nelson Burr registered for the 1850 census in Lenox, but a short time later he moved his family to Rock Island County, Illinois. There Dale's grandfather, John Percival Burr, was born in 1860. Levi, who was fourteen years older than John P., spent a couple of weeks in the Union Army at the very end of the Civil War, and then hightailed it farther west. Nelson continued to farm land near Edington, Illinois, until John was nearly grown, but he had not given up his hope of something better, or his urge to keep westering. In the summer of 1879, when he was nearly sixty years old, he moved the family again, this time to settle on 160 acres near Lone Tree, Iowa.

Their glowing reports about Lone Tree soon brought Levi from Nebraska, and gave Nelson the satisfaction of having both his sons farming at his side. Nor was this his sole satisfaction in old age, for he lived to see the ruin of the large English farmers who had swallowed up his ancestors. In the five decades since the Burrs emigrated, the surviving large English farmers had gone deeply in debt to buy new machinery, expand drainage, and otherwise increase productivity. Ironically, their often dramatic successes only hastened their downfall, for the enclosures created a popular majority whose interests were diametrically opposed to their own.

The urban workers wanted cheap food, as did their employers, who were eager to maintain their competitive edge in world markets. The primacy of urban interests was evident as early as 1846, when Parliament under Tory Prime Minister Robert Peel repealed the Corn Laws, which had protected English agriculture from foreign competition. Before the century was out, this change destroyed thousands of English farmers, for like the American farm crisis of the 1980s, the late nineteenth century was a period of mammoth food surpluses and falling food prices.

During the 1870s, North American grain coming off the Great Plains drove the world price of wheat down to levels unknown since before 1700. During the 1880s, the cost of a loaf of bread fell by half. We tend to think today of Denmark and Switzerland as always having been dairying nations, but actually each grew its own wheat until American competition made this impossible and their farmers were forced to establish specialty niches. The English tried to do the same, but found that the Americans could sell cheese for two pence a pound less than any English cheese maker.

There followed a great milk glut, which decimated prices in the commodity that many English farmers were betting would take them through the crisis. Thousands of the supposedly smartest and most progressive farmers in England lost everything, and were forced off the farm as land ownership contracted still further. Between 1870 and the beginning of the twentieth century, seven hundred thousand more English farmers and farm workers emigrated to the corners of the globe.

Nelson Burr, who with his sons helped heap the killing American agricultural overproduction a little higher around the necks of his English counterparts, probably felt a certain sad satisfaction in the workings of fate. But then he was an old man. His American-born sons were not concerned with the ancient grievances that came over, like oddly styled clothes, from the old country. They thought they had put all that behind them.

During the early years of this century, John P. Burr commissioned a photographer to record the material grandeur he had attained during a lifetime of farming near Lone Tree. The resulting picture, which Burr paid to have published in *Leading Events in Johnson County History,* contains no people, no livestock, and somewhat surprisingly, no farm buildings.

Instead, it is a view across at least a half-acre of neatly mowed lawn to a white, two-story Iowa farmhouse with black shutters and a gracious shade tree bending over one eave. The bay window on the ground floor and the glass balls on the lightning rods above the roof indicate that this is a house of substance.

Behind it, and partly visible at one side, is the house that Nelson built when the Burrs first moved to Iowa three decades before. Low, dark, and utterly plain, except for print curtains hanging in the windows, the old place stands as a reminder of the heroic past, and a measure of the progress of the most recent generation of Burrs.

The most telling thing about the photo, however, is on the front porch under the bright new house's Victorian filigree. Here one rocking chair sits a little forlornly on the wide porch. The inadequacy of this convenience in a household of eight, plus hired men, shows John P.'s hand clearly. Not only was the reigning Burr patriarch a yeoman worker, but he liked to keep the rest of the family busy too. There were not too many evenings spent loafing around the porch complaining about the gnats at the Burr house.

Despite the fact that he was a wealthy man and prominent citizen, John P. expected his kids to develop an early understanding of the necessity of honest toil. He wouldn't stint on giving them a good foundation and good materials to work with, but work they must. And so Vernon Burr, John P.'s second son and Dale's father, was, sent to high school in Iowa City rather than the one-room schoolhouse in the county. An enterprising lad, he earned the money for his train rides back and forth to school by shooting rabbits and selling them in town for twenty-five cents each.

Vernon had a spirited streak too. He owned the high-wheeled old bicycle that hung for many years in the Burr barn, as well as a loud string of big raw-boned motorcycles. He even had a cut-out on the exhaust of his Buick, which Dale used to beg him to kick in when they were out riding without Hilda. At the same time, Vernon followed closely in his nineteenth-century father's footsteps. Like his father, he inherited a good Iowa farm, and like his father, he expanded the size of the family holdings substantially; like his father, he attained that pinnacle of rural American respectability, a directorship at the local bank, and like his father, he thought of himself as "first, last, and always, a farmer."

A squat, bald barrel of a man, with massive forearms and a quick rolling gait, Vernon liked to say, "I got a good start, but I made it anyway." As common in manner as he was in appearance, he would sometimes hitchhike into town for a spare part instead of driving one of his several vehicles. He justified this in terms of meeting people and picking up news, but the family was not entirely convinced. His daughter, Ruth, teased him about his unwillingness to spend a dime for a copy of the Sunday newspaper until it became something of a family joke. Oh, Dad, she would say.

Neighbors testify that Vernon and his wife, Hilda, were not much for casual socializing. The family was the social focus of their lives, and virtually all-encompassing. "We were never let out of Mom and Dad's sight," Ruth recently recalled of her and Dale's upbringing. "When they went somewhere at night, we'd go with them. There wasn't such a thing as a 'baby-sitter' in those days," she added with a laugh. Like their own parents, Hilda and Vernon were strict no-nonsense disciplinarians who demanded a lot of their two children. "It wasn't the kind of family where there was a lot of physical touching," Ruth said, "but you knew you were loved."

A favorite family outing when Ruth and Dale were young was the annual trip to the Iowa State Fair in Des Moines, which in those days of dirt roads and balloon tires assumed the proportions of an epic journey. Generally, the 250-mile round-trip required spending one night on the road each way, with a tarp strung over the car and everybody bedded down around the sides of the vehicle. Dale loved the covered-wagon-like romance of the trip, but the best part was the fair itself. The encamped farmers always awoke to the pre-dawn cry of "Oh, Joe, where's your mule?" with which pranksters perpetuated the memory of a long-lost mule. And in the evening, boys like Dale would drift off to sleep to the sound of music wafting over from luridly lit late-night scenes along the carny.

It was here that Dale probably first heard the thundering hooves of racehorses, and felt the rising mix of expectation and dread that pulls the racetrack crowd to its feet. There were dances and concerts and, even more intriguing for an adolescent male, the frankly self-improving (as well as sometimes equally frankly bogus) curios on display for a dime. Cousin Bob Berry recalls how one year Dale was the only kid in the family who got to see what purported to be a pickled whale in a tank. All of the other Burr cousins had already failed to get their fathers to take them to see this amazing spectacle when Vernon decided to indulge his boy's curiosity. Later, the other boys hung with rapturous revulsion on Dale's description of the creature's embryolike appendages and ashy, convoluted hide.

That baby gray whale made an especially big impression on Dale because apart from the county and state fairs and a few hunting and fishing trips, his world was pretty much circumscribed by the land and people of Lone Tree. As a young boy, he rode his white pony to Lincoln Township School #7, the one-room schoolhouse down the lane from where he lived. The teachers—generally a succession of young, unmarried women—changed over the years, but the students remained the same. It was common for a group of children to stay together all the way through school. This promoted a familial feeling that was reenforced by the children's traditional chore of lighting the school's pot-bellied stove every morning.

Later Dale attended high school in town, but when most of his contemporaries went off to war or the munitions factories after Pearl Harbor, he stayed behind on the farm with an exemption for crucial war-related work. Dale was no more crucial to the war effort than the dozens of Johnson County farm boys from his class who were drafted, of course. The difference, as more than a few people noted, was that he was Vernon Burr's son. Popular sentiment was hostile to individuals who avoided the military, and more than a few farm boys who stayed home found their barns painted yellow while they slept. This never happened to Dale, but there were people around Lone Tree who would not talk to him for decades after because he did not serve during World War II.

In truth, Dale Burr was a great service to both his country and family during the war. With virtually every able-bodied man away overseas, it got to the point where Dale almost seemed to live in the fields. Although farmers were not in any mortal danger, the work was physically punishing. They hayed for nearly three months straight in those days, and even though Dale always took the position of the stacker, which was the most grueling, they all found their bodies giving out. Vernon developed an aggravated collection of chronic injuries, and his hands callused into horny hooks that cracked painfully. The Burrs' one hired man, John Johnson, began to slather his hands with Watkins Salve every night. Then he would have Hilda Burr pull white cotton gloves on each hand, and tie them at the wrists with string.

It was also during the war years that Dale's relationship with his father took the form it was to maintain throughout the remainder of Vernon's long life. Although he joked that he wanted to be "tall like my Uncle Bob," Dale had always idolized his father. Now, under the pressure of war production, Vernon made Dale field boss of the family's amalgamated holdings. While other Iowa farm boys were dropping bombs on Japan, Dale Burr was learning to farm bigger and leaner than most people around Lone Tree had thought of yet. By the end of World War II, Dale was probably the best field farmer in Lincoln Township.

Vernon, for his part, was as financially shrewd and well connected a farmer as you were likely to find in Johnson County. A director of the Lone Tree Bank, like his father before him, he had access to money and inside information on the financial situation of many of his fellow farmers in the county. Together, Vernon and Dale proved a productive powerhouse. The two worked very comfortably in harness, but there was never any doubt about who was leading. Keith Forbes, Dale's brother-in-law, recalled how Dale and Vernon farmed: "Dale'd go up there [to Vernon's home place] in the morning, and he and Vernon would go over what needed doing that day, and then Dale'd do it."

In those days, the Burrs ran a classic diversified farming operation. They grew corn and grain, selling some, and feeding some to their numerous and varied animals, which included cattle, sheep, hogs, and poultry. Vernon and Dale had experience with large-scale growing for the government during World War II, but their enterprise remained based on a variety of activities, privately transacted. Even though their operation had grown large, they still followed the ancient principle of the diversified yeoman economy: Don't put all your eggs in one basket.

The Burrs made so much money during World War II that Vernon was actually a little at a loss as to what to do with it. Finally he decided he would buy some more land. His idea was not to increase the holdings he and Dale worked, but to lease the land to another operator, thus establishing a steady, long-term source of cash income for the future. And so in the late 1940s, Vernon paid cash for over a square mile of Iowa farmland, 660 acres, about thirty miles south of Lone Tree, outside the town of Columbus Junction, near the verdant banks of the Iowa River.

The purchase of this expansive, rolling farm put Vernon in very elite company. Most farmers could not even afford to dream of owning that much land—let alone pay cash for it. The fact that someone like Vernon Burr could amass a thousand acres of prime Iowa farmland showed what hard work and a level head could accomplish. In this sense, the Burrs' success was a reflection of the best in America.

But the Burrs' success was also built on the destruction of other farmers. Vernon Burr's Columbus Junction purchase was an example of the increasing concentration of American farm ownership that was forcing hundreds of thousands of small farmers off the land every year, just as had occurred previously in England.

For generations, the Burrs' competence and drive had kept them among the winners, but the shakeout was far from over. In fact, the pace of the American enclosures was accelerating.

3

"One thing I'll never forget is making hay," said Keith Forbes. "I hayed with them every summer. Now, Ruth's dad and Dale never carried water in the field when they worked. Never! Those people could work all day without a drink. And if they did take any water, it was in a glass jug that sat out in the heat and got warm.

"I remember one real hot afternoon, Emily came out with a big pitcher of iced tea with lemon—you know, with the dew just dripping off it. They didn't want to stop. They were never ones to stop when they were working, not even for a minute, but she came out and talked them into it. And gosh, I really appreciated that."

With her lustrous black hair and smooth skin showing at the neck of her breezy summer dress, Emily Burr was not the sort of vision you met in the fields of Iowa every day. She had a stylish presence, and her graces were particularly evident as she sipped tea briefly in the shade of the wagon with the sweat-drenched men.

"A real looker," as a schoolmate who had once dated her recalled with a flash in his eyes a half-century later, Emily took the Burrs by storm during the last days of World War II. She had a lot of energy, and a way of appreciating the things people said that made them seem special. With a cheerful suggestion here and a deft bit of homemaking there, she induced the Burrs to change some of their ways until even Vernon was stopping work to drink iced tea.

Dale was crazy for her. He did not have to say anything for that to be clear. Sometimes he almost gave the impression of a kid who couldn't believe his own good fortune. His bride was a head-turning beauty who was the daughter of a banker from a neighboring town. She was bright, cheerful, and fun, but also hard-working and devout. A year older than Dale and town-reared in a much more self-consciously genteel atmosphere, Emily also carried the cachet of sophistication.

"She came from the prominent family in Wilton Junction," recalled her sister-in-law, Ruth Forbes. "Her father was the town banker and very religious. She and her two sisters were brought up very strict." The daughter of Arthur "A.J." Wacker and Emilia Wilhelmina Grunder, Emily grew up in a large white, slate-roofed mansion on Maurer Street, where the Wackers owned an entire block near the top of the hill. The family compound was buttressed by her father's three-story manse on one corner, and her uncle Herbert Wacker's even larger turreted affair on the other corner, with Emily's grandmother's place in between.

Wilton Junction had long been a center for German-speaking people, many of them Protestants, unlike the Bohemian Catholics who settled around Lone Tree. At the turn of the century, it had a college (the Wilton German-English college), an "opera house" (actually a hundred-foot-long hall upstairs in the Scott & Blanchard building), and its own steam electrical generator to power the municipal street-lights (which were turned off every night at eleven). Located at the junction of the mainline of the Rock Island Railroad and the spur line to Muscatine, Wilton Junction was larger than Lone Tree, with more diversions.

The heart of the town remained agricultural, though. The seemingly endless fields of corn and beans began only a few blocks north of Emily's house, and the Wacker compound itself was near the cabin of Christian Marolf, Wilton Junction's first settler. As a young girl, Emily heard family friends reminisce about how in the early days the prairie fires swept out of the south and the settlers had to plow furrows around their cabins and barns to save them from the flames. Even though the Wackers were not farmers, their business—like everyone else's in town—was dependent on farming.

Emily's grandfather, John H. Wacker, founded a thriving blacksmith and wagon shop that grew into the town's main farm-implement dealer. In March 1898, J. H. Wacker and Co. sold twenty plows, seventeen harrows, four disks, a few seeders, and one stalk cutter, all of the horse-drawn variety. Corn planters were in great demand in May, followed closely by corn cultivators, of which two types were favored: walking models at fifteen dollars and the "New Deere Rider" at twenty-three. The most expensive item in the store at the time was the "New Moline" wagon, which sold for fifty-five dollars, and might cost even more if the customer chose options like extra sideboards advertised as the "tip-top box."

After the turn of the century, the implements became increasingly expensive, and the sales techniques more inventive. In 1929, when Emily was eight, the Wacker clan was abuzz with a dramatic new tractor sales promotion scheme. A.J.'s brother, Herbert, who was also mayor of Wilton for many years, had cooked up a plan to send a brand-new Farmall tractor through the countryside to plow corn for free. The idea was to convince farmers that a tractor was superior to horses, even though it cost much more to own and operate.

As a youth, most of Emily's life centered on a few-block area in Wilton and the activities there involving family, school, and the Zion Lutheran Church, where her father was a pillar. She attended public school a block and a half from her home. In high school, she proved a good student, athletic and popular like her sisters. She had many admirers, but the stern discipline of her father kept the serious suitors at bay, and prevented any lasting relationships from forming before all the eligible young men went overseas to war. Emily, who was the last person anyone expected to be an old maid, found herself living at home in her twenties (a spinsterly age for women at that time in rural America). Bright enough to go to college and capable enough to work, she could have gone down to the station and caught a train for Chicago or Denver, but she was too good a daughter.

A.J. and Emilia had very clear ideas of what was appropriate for their children. Certainly common working was out of the question. A.J. felt that it might lead to corruption. He was adamant that young women should be cheerful and chaste, embodying Christian virtue, especially with eligible young men from the few wealthier families he deemed acceptable. The sort of man who was accustomed to setting the terms in life, he did not want to leave anything to chance regarding his daughters. Emily obeyed her father's wishes, but by the summer of 1944, when she was twenty-two, she was beginning to wonder if she was going to end up safe and sorry.

Dale and Emily first met that year at the old West Liberty Fair on a warm night under an Iowa moon. It was during the height of World War II, when everything exciting and everyone interesting seemed far away, and they were both surprised to find someone so young and good-looking among the old men and children, soldiers on crutches, and girls waiting for their heroic sweethearts to return from overseas. The initial attraction deepened over the following months, for despite their superficial differences, they were similar in many respects. Both were the product of strict, insular, and affluent families; both were good children who had distinguished themselves by obedience to strong parents; both were deeply rooted in the Iowa countryside and Midwestern culture.

They seemed to understand each other quickly, as if they had known each other for years. Perhaps even more important, both A.J. Wacker and Vernon Burr were amenable toward a union of their two families and fortunes. In fact, the more they learned about each other, and each other's children, the more they warmed toward Dale and Emily's romance. Each saw in the other the sort of family he thought would assure his child a good mate and a financially secure future. And so in November 1945, Emily and Dale were married in a lavish ceremony in Wilton Junction. One person who was in attendance remembers that an intense hailstorm battered the church while the minister preached on and on for nearly an hour, as if determined to outlast the passion of nature.

The couple honeymooned in Des Moines, where Dale bought himself a new shotgun, a Remington model 31. Soon Dale and Emily returned to the 160-acre place that

Vernon gave them to get started. The George Reiland property was located about a mile south of Vernon's place, but Dale had known it for many years, since the one-room school he had attended was located there. Vernon had purchased it during the depths of the Great Depression for the rock-bottom price of ninety dollars an acre. It was a nice farm, with good land, a beautiful white farmhouse, and an assortment of outbuildings. Emily immediately set about decorating the house with items from her parents' home. "When Emily and Dale got married and set up housekeeping, she refused to take anything out of Vernon and Hilda's house," recalled a member of the family. "Her mother lived in this monster house in Wilton that was full of old things. She had all the antiques from there she needed to fill her new house."

Lone Tree, or LONE Tree, as residents pronounce it, is notable for the plainness and lack of ostentation shown by its wealthiest farmers. Nearby West Branch might dress up for the tourists streaming through Herbert Hoover's birthplace just off I-80, but Lone Tree does not put on airs for anyone. Much of the land around Lone Tree is actually better than that around West Branch, but in Lone Tree it is more the local custom to put the money "in the ground," as the expression goes, than to show it off in town. "Most of the big farmers drive older vehicles," observed a longtime Lone Tree resident, "and if you see someone with a flashy car, you can bet they are in hock up to their eyes on it." For this reason, there was a little uncertainty in town about what to expect from the daughter of a German banker who had probably never milked a cow in her life.

For her part, Emily was a little concerned about Lone Tree. Dale was good to her—they all were—but at the beginning she was particularly aware of her isolation. Lone

Tree was still the sort of solitary stick the name suggested, lacking Wilton Junction's size or the steel pulse of the transcontinental rail line. To make matters worse, their home was more than three miles outside of town itself. The nearest neighbors on the sparsely populated gravel spur road were a quarter-mile away. It was not easy to stroll next door for a chat, but in time Emily made friends with a group of women from the neighborhood known jokingly as "the robin bunch." A neighbor recalled that one member of the group was always phoning another to report seeing some bird, compare recipes, or just chat.

Emily also joined the service organizations like the Lone Tree Women's Club. "She always had a smile on her face," recalled a friend, "and just as soon as you'd see her, she'd be ready to sit down and talk." Said another, "Emily was good at everything—cooking, decorating, you name it—and had a way of making everything look easy." Male friends tend to remark on her cooking. "She was one of the finest ladies and finest cooks around," said one. Desserts, particularly pies, were a specialty of Emily's, as were chicken fried steaks and multilayered Jell-O salads. In time, she even developed a reputation for such Lone Tree exotica as Chinese food. "I remember Emily worked with the girls all one winter on sweet-and-sour pork," recalled the mother of a girl in Emily's Prairie Master 4-H group. She added with a chuckle, "I believe they finally did get it in the end."

What filled her life more than anything else were her children. Emily and Dale's first, John Nelson Burr, was born almost exactly a year from the day they were married. Sheila arrived two years later, followed by Julia in 1955. All three were happy, healthy kids who would make any parent, or grandparent, proud. In fact, the elder Burrs and Wackers were delighted with their grandchildren. A relative recalled that Hilda Burr's excitement over the arrival of the new generation almost overcame her natural Scandinavian reticence. "Hilda used to speak proudly of their shorthorns, but after the grandchildren started coming along, she never talked about the cattle anymore. Then it was always the grandkids this, the grandkids that."

Emily shared her mother-in-law's deep commitment to the family. She was the kind of mother who was always there to pick up the girls when they got off the bus, and she drove John on his first date when he was still too young to get a driver's permit. The miles she logged around little Lone Tree with three active children were substantial, but she was much more than a chauffeur. The emotional heart of the family, she set the tone for all their numerous activities as she wove them together. All the kids, and Dale too, took strength from her. She could be demanding, but never mean. Friendly and calm, she always seemed to have time to listen and help. Those who knew her came to appreciate her, for Keith Forbes with his glass of iced tea was just one of many who were touched by her kindness.

More social than her husband, Emily especially enjoyed the card parties traditionally held every winter after the year's fieldwork was completed. She and Dale were part of a group of six couples who had been getting together for thirty years to play euchre. They would set the table with their best china, and each woman would bring a favorite dish. Conversations were warm and jocular, and many of the jokes well-worn. Dale played euchre competently, but he was not in Emily's class. The same might be said for Dale and Emily as conversationalists. There was never any hostility evident between them, though. In fact, Dale and Emily spent more time together than many couples who have been married forty years.

Friends were struck by the fact that they often shopped together, both for groceries and antiques. After the girls moved out, Emily took over one of the empty bedrooms upstairs and turned it into a workshop. She and Dale would visit antique stores and auctions in the area, looking for good pieces that needed attention. When they found the cherry table or oak bed they were looking for, they would haul it home, and Emily would go to work on it. She was quite proficient at such restoration work, and a friend recalls "she always had someone in mind" for every piece.

Yet Emily's activities could not entirely obscure the return of the loneliness she had felt three decades before. A close friend believes that beneath her calm, controlled exterior, "she was not a happy woman." Beginning when John Burr went away to college at Iowa State University in Ames, the number of empty rooms in the house increased steadily. Sheila married and moved to far-off Rogers, Arkansas, to start a new life with her husband. Finally, even Emily's baby, Julia, left home to start a career as a teacher.

Then, just as the kids' leaving home was diminishing her role in the family, circumstances were elevating Dale. He now had more demands on his attention than ever before, and less time for her. Although Dale remained unequivocably faithful, there was more emotional distance between him and Emily.

In truth, Emily was not the last great passion of Dale Burr's life, nor did she share it.

Friends say Dale's interest in horses dated from the early 1950s when one of Emily's sisters was looking for a place to board her mare. Dale and Emily volunteered to let her keep it at their place, and so one day they brought the horse out in a trailer.

Before long, Dale started acquiring quarter horses of his own. He did not use the animals for work around the farm, or even ride them for pleasure. The only one in the family who rode extensively was Julia, who won numerous ribbons with Burr horses, just as her older brother had done with Burr cattle. Dale kept horses because he enjoyed having them around, just like the pheasants.

The real growth in the Burrs' stable did not occur until the late 1970s, after Julia had left home. That was when Vernon was struck by a paralyzing stroke. Vernon lived on for several years more, but he never walked again, and as he neared eighty he was finally forced to relinquish control of the family farm enterprise to his son. The transition was nearly as swift as the wait had been long, but Dale seemed to have reached the point for which his entire life had been preparing him.

Dale did not make any big changes immediately, but farmers began to notice what was to prove a characteristic habit with fieldwork. Rather than compact the soil, which had a slightly higher clay content on the Burr place than elsewhere in Lincoln Township, he stayed out of the fields until later in the spring than some of his neighbors. Vernon used to get around this problem to an extent by using a Caterpillar tractor, which spread the weight as widely as possible. Even in his old age he relished getting out on his Cat first thing in the spring, saying with a characteristic laugh, "I'm as good as any man when I'm on a tractor."

After Dale took over managing the family enterprise, he got rid of the Cat, preferring to wait until conventional equipment could get into the fields. A lot of farmers never gave a second thought to soil compaction of this sort, but Dale was more conscientious than most. He knew that it was better for the land if he did not plant until the ground had dried out a little more, so he decided to take that as his guide. For that reason, it was often nearly June before Dale got his crop planted and November before he could get the harvest wrapped up. This was late for the area around Lone Tree, and ensured some loss of quality due to weather damage. Other farmers figured the Burrs were big enough to pay that tithe to conservation, though.

A more obvious change of Dale's was getting rid of the cattle. The sheep had already been phased out, and now shorthorns—including the family milk cow—were sold off. The Burrs were not alone in getting out of beef during the mid-1970s. Many farmers did likewise as American agriculture underwent a nationwide shift toward specialization. By the late 1970s the Burrs primarily produced only commercial corn, beans, and pork. Gone were the spread of endeavor and the subsistence crops that used to insulate them from the failure of any one cash crop. Meanwhile, the russet-and-white shorthorn cattle that had dotted the Burrs' fields for generations were replaced with glistening racehorses.

Since Dale had neither the time nor the inclination to care for his stable, he hired others to do a lot of it. Jim Hopps, from outside Muscatine, and Charlie Boerjan in Iowa City helped him some, but most of the work with Dale's horses was performed by Don and Gerald Rayner, the twin sons of Dale's horse mentor, the late Ralph "Blinky" Rayner. The Rayners broke and trained Dale's animals. They also raced them for him at "bush" tracks in places like Hastings, Nebraska. A friend recalls that Dale had some winners among his horses, but added that the victory money often did not cover the expenses of a weekend of racing.

Small and informal as the name suggests, bush-track racing differs from thoroughbred horse racing in the length of the race, the breed of horses used, and the fact that pari-mutuel betting is not allowed. All these factors combine to give bush-track events more the feeling of a swap meet than the Preakness. It is possible to bet the night before, however, in the "Calcutta." Under this system, supporters of the horses running get together ahead of time to put money on the race. They bid whatever it takes in an open auction to place their name on the horse of their choice. The highest bidder on each horse has exclusive claim to that animal for betting purposes, and all the money goes into a pot. The next day, the person who put his name on the winning horse gets the pot, usually around two hundred dollars.

After a few years, Dale moved up to pari-mutuel racing at tracks like Moline Downs in East Moline, Illinois. Purses were bigger here, as were the possible profits of futuras and associated breeding schemes. But then, the costs were higher too. One horse-racing associate said he knew that Dale lost several thousand dollars when a quarter horse track in Illinois went bankrupt. Bob Berry remembered that he and his wife went with Dale to Moline Downs in the Quad Cities once in the early 1980s. They ate at the track and made a day of it that was only slightly dampened by the fact that Dale's horses lost. Emily's presence made it an occasion to remember, for she did not always go along with Dale on his horse forays. In fact, the horses were something of a bone of contention between them.

Dale spent as much as $2,500 to breed his mares to top studs like Poco Blue Rip and Moon Control, even though Emily did not always approve. A neighbor, Harold Schuessler, remembers Emily commenting to him one spring when Dale was gone all day getting a mare bred that "he should be here planting corn." Dale, for his part, felt he had earned the horses. He worked harder than most contemporary

Americans knew how, and had been doing it for nearly forty years. The horses were his only major recreation. "That's my beer, cigarettes, and bowling," he once told a relative, and it was true. Dale did not smoke or drink, did not hang out in town or go to movies. He used to bowl in Muscatine, but gave it up years ago. He knew the animals were costing him money, but then, what recreation did not cost money? You could spend fifty dollars on a night out in Cedar Rapids.

Dale was not going to let Emily's objections stop him from running the horses as he saw fit. If that meant he had to go to the track alone, he was willing. Emily began going to church alone more too. Members of the parish of Our Redeemer Lutheran Church in Iowa City noticed this, and remember that Emily was less inclined to stay and talk after service. Joking about "Emily's Restaurant," she said she had to get home to cook for the men. A friend recalls her saying a little sadly once as she excused herself to go home one Sunday, "The men work so hard." Privately, it appears she was increasingly concerned over how the farm was being managed.

Emily had been raised in a milieu that both taught her to accept male authority and gave her an unusually deep understanding of farm financing. Now this legacy began to trouble her, for she heard John and Dale discussing big deals that did not seem to add up. Emily knew her son had been losing money, and she knew Dale had pledged land as collateral on loans for John. She suggested cutting back on the horses, but this only seemed to spur Dale in the other direction. By the early 1980s, he had around fifty-five brood mares on the place. It was not hard to see that Dale's horses were costing more than the shorthorns he had gotten rid of a few years before, and returning nothing in income. The horse issue was like a rope between Dale and Emily that drew taut as larger problems overcame the American farm economy.

All around them the countryside was gripped by the worst farm crisis in fifty years. Neither Dale nor his neighbors (who all grew the same crops) could escape the fact that commodity prices were falling through the floor, due to tremendous overproduction, surpluses, and cheap foreign competition. In 1983, for instance, wheat sold for $5.25 a bushel. In 1984, it brought only $3.46. For over half a century the U.S. Department of Agriculture has figured the buying power of farmers compared to the period 1910–14. In 1984, parity hovered around 58. That is, farmers had 58 percent of the buying power their forebears had seven decades before. The other part of the vise that held the farmer in the early 1980s was the staggering debt load they had assumed over the previous thirty years, which greatly increased their cost of doing business. In 1950, total U.S. farm debt stood at $12.5 billion and net farm income was $19 billion. By 1984, the debt had soared to $215 billion and net income in constant dollars dropped to $5.4 billion.

The Department of Agriculture officially classified about 17 percent of the nation's farmers as "stressed" or "vulnerable" financially, but Iowa Sate University economists estimated the distress to be much more extensive. A third of the state's farmers faced severe financial trouble in 1984, and another third were nearly at that point. Towns started losing their implement dealers, their retail stores, their populations, their schools. Finally, rural banks, which had heavily backed and even solicited the loans, began to go under. About fifty federally insured farm banks folded during 1985, as did uninsured banks like the one in Bloomfield, Iowa, where depositors got ten cents on the dollar. Nationwide, the Farm Credit System, which held about one-third of the nation's farm debt, lost more than $2.5 billion that year, and was in what Iowa State economist Neil Harl called "an extremely precarious position."

In Iowa practically everyone knew somebody like Jim White of Pleasantville, the two-time former Polk County Corn Champion who was forced into a Chapter 11 federal bankruptcy declaration because he extended his credit to his sons so they could get started farming. They sensed the terrible pressure this put on men scattered out across the countryside. "I have personally dealt with farmers on the phone who had a loaded shotgun and were ready to get in the pickup and go down to the bank," said Dan Levitas of Prairiefire, a Des Moines–based hotline for troubled farmers. Pete Zevenbergen, director of the Linn County, Iowa, Community Mental Health Center, said another farmer, the son of a farmer who died of a heart attack during foreclosure, had a loaded gun and circled a bank in a vehicle for two days "waiting for the banker to come to work."

Attacks on bankers had, in fact, already occurred in two states. In September 1983, James Jenks, a former farmer who had been foreclosed on by the Buffalo State Bank in Ruthton, Minnesota, lured the bank president and the loan officer out to Jenks's old place and murdered them with the aid of his teenage son. Jenks, whose story is chronicled in Andrew Malcolm's *Final Harvest,* later committed suicide. In October 1984, debt-ridden farmer Arthur Kirk was shot and killed by the Nebraska State Patrol SWAT team after he opened fire on deputies attempting to notify him that the Grand Island Northwest Bank was taking his property for nonpayment of loans. The Jenks and Kirk tragedies were products of the farm crisis, but in both cases the perpetrators were fringe characters and not the sort of successful farmers whose failure was so symptomatic of the farm crisis of the 1980s.

Then, in the fall of 1985, three first-rate Iowa farmers committed suicide in one seven-day stretch, September 20 through 26. They were Gordon Geiken of Vinton (a big farmer and banker who was depressed over what he was having to do to neighbors as bank director), Marvin Reed of Iowa Falls (a substantial beef producer and modern operator who had been financially ruined), and Steven Meeker of Letts (the son of a large hog producer who was depressed about his father's financial woes). All were bright, hardworking, and well liked. In short, they were exactly the type of person who would traditionally be expected to succeed in Middle America.

More and more, however, psychologists were pegging this type as the most likely to be pushed over the brink by their financial destruction. "If you were a go-getter, the person who rises to the top, the person who has used all the techniques possible to make it not only big, but big as possible, then you have a certain belief system that's been working," said Joan Blundall of the Northern Iowa Mental Health Center. She added that these days "that belief system doesn't fit in with reality."

On farms all across America, proud people were sitting around kitchen tables staring at ruin. Their whole world seemed to be quaking, and if they lost their grip, they would be cast adrift to . . . what? Terror of the unknown —as much as the particulars of their problems—was what drove some to bare their despair.

Around noon on Saturday, November 30, Keith Forbes swiveled around in his chair at his desk in the kitchen of his home between Lone Tree and Iowa City, and squinted at the truck that pulled up in the drive. He slid his glasses down off his forehead and scrutinized the car more closely, before announcing to Ruth a visit from her brother, Dale, and his wife, Emily.

"It was unusual that the two of them came over here together," he said. "They just never, never did that. Dale wasn't one for talk, but for five hours they poured out their hearts. They just unloaded the whole thing—all the problems they were having debt-wise." Dale was calm and quiet, but Emily was "nearly hysterical," he said. Normally immaculate, she had her gray-streaked hair tied up with an old bandanna, and her clothes were disheveled.

"He kept a-tellin' us about his debt," said Forbes. "He kept saying, 'Oh, I got a hell of a debt.' " Dale talked on and on about his tangled financial difficulties, revealing that he had borrowed heavily from the bank accounts of his mother, who lived in a nearby rest home. The main thing on his mind, though, was the recent hassle with the Hills Bank over money from corn he grew and "sealed" with the government for $23,000. He said that the Hills Bank "was getting really rough" with him. He added that he could not pay the $39,000 due on another loan the Hills Bank had just called the day before. Apparently, he thought he could lose the farm to foreclosure as early as December 6. "They sure got me now," Dale said. "I can't seal nothing and I can't sell nothing."

At one point, Dale announced, "I'm going to the bank Monday and tell them they can have it all—my land, everything. I'm finished." Walking across the kitchen to his cluttered rolltop desk, Keith Forbes picked up the phone and began dialing the number of a family attorney. Forbes thought he might be able to cut Dale's incessant gloom with some helpful advice, but Dale persuaded him to hang up before the call went through. "I don't have nearly enough to pay his fee," Dale explained, adding that he was running out of feed for his beloved quarter horses. He said he had only fourteen bales of hay left, or enough to last until Christmas. Emily said, "I'm sixty-four years old and for the first time in my life I don't have money for groceries." The Forbeses remember Emily repeating several times, "They'll put him in jail. I know they will."

Dale did not deny her assertion. "He just talked and talked and talked," Ruth recalled. "Then he got up and sat over there on the bench. He didn't say any more. He just clammed up." As the Burrs were leaving, Emily turned to Ruth. "In a demanding or begging way she said, 'Come down this week,' " Ruth remembered. Keith Forbes thought that Dale seemed better when he left that night. "He really perked up. When he left here I thought we had it turned around, that he'd get some advice and get refinanced and have the thing going all right." Forbes contacted the Farmers Home Administration (FmHA) on Dale's behalf Monday morning and learned that the federal agency that serves as the farmers' "lender of last resort" might be able to help Dale. Alerted by his brother-in-law, Dale went into the Hills Bank the next day, December 2, to obtain the financial information he needed for the FmHA loan application.

He met with an FmHA representative in nearby West Branch later that week, and was told that they would try to have an answer for him by the following Tuesday, December 10. In the meantime, Dale borrowed five hundred dollars from his daughter Julia in Eau Claire. He also visited the Farmers and Merchants Savings Bank in Lone Tree several times that week attempting to secure loans, and on Saturday he met with an officer of the Columbus Junction State Bank. According to a relative who talked to the bank official, Dale said he wanted the money for his son, John. He said, "I want to money up my boy." The bank officer reportedly responded, "Dale, John is broke." Later that day, Dale visited neighbor Leslie Parizek to see if anything could be done to stop the forfeiture proceedings Parizek had brought against John Burr on the old Parizek place.

The situation was an emotionally difficult one for Parizek. By his own account, there had never been a harsh word spoken between him and Dale. He had been delighted to sell the eighty acres across the road to John Burr in 1982. And even though John's lack of payments had forced the Parizeks to start forfeiture proceedings late that summer, they had always been willing to work things out so John could keep the farm. He told Dale he had in fact just received a check from John for $8,000, which was essentially to pay interest. But unfortunately, the check had bounced. Parizek said he had contacted the bank, and been told that he would never receive another dime from John Burr in payment for his old place because the bank had complete control of the younger Burr's finances and would not allow him to pay any more to the Parizeks.

What Leslie Parizek was telling his old friend was that it was already all over. The banks had taken control of his son, and they would have him too in a matter of days. Then, completely bound and powerless, he would be reduced to pauperism and public ridicule for the profit of the banks, which were the cause of so many of his problems. The people of Johnson County, who never forgot anything, would forever say Dale was the weak link in the chain of Burrs, the one who lost it all, all that he was given, not just for himself, but all those generations to come. They would pity him, and not just him, but Emily too. Dale worked in the fields most of the afternoon and into the night. Back and forth he went across the somber landscape in his big red combine, harvesting corn and beans, and thinking.

Sometimes trying to think clearly was like trying to plow a straight furrow in April muck, though. He would form a thought in his mind and begin to consider it, only to find himself lurching off line. He was exhausted and had begun to lose weight. Friends were beginning to notice the fatigue in his eyes, even though he still maintained the old facade. Dale stopped by Harold Schuessler's one evening during the first week of December to ask if he could bring some wagons of corn across part of the Schuessler place. "We sat here in the kitchen and had a real jolly chat," said Schuessler. Likewise, cousin Robert Berry recalled that Dale was typically affable when he and Emily came over to see slides of the Berrys' recent trip to Africa on the evening of Thursday, December 5.

Dale worked until nearly midnight on December 8 trying to get the crops harvested. The weather report was not good, and so he kept at it, hauling wagonload after wagonload out of the fields as the north wind bit at his back. As usual, he worked alone. Perhaps because of this, and the fact that it was a Sunday—the day that he used to say he'd die before he'd work—Dale's thoughts turned dark. Many acres still remained to be harvested when he finally called it quits that night, but it appears he had reached a personal decision. Even though he had several weeks' worth of hay left, he killed five of his horses (including a favorite buckskin colt) and left their bodies in the corral to half drift over with blowing snow.

The morning of Monday, December 9, dawned cold and cloudy with a light wind out of the northeast. At breakfast Dale told John his plans for the day. He was going to the

Hills Bank, after which he would stop by the Siever Place, bring the tractor up, and haul grain. John said he was going to work on the hogs at his grandmother's farm, and headed up there a few minutes later. Dale did not set out on his business of the day immediately, though. Sensing that his mood was not good, Emily called and politely canceled out of the regular bridge club meeting she had planned to attend.

Even good friends noticed that Emily was seeing people less. Usually, she would sit in the car and talk with her neighbor Doris Schuessler for a good half hour or more when Doris dropped her off from some errand. "Those women really loved to talk," recalled Doris's husband, Harold. Less than a week before, though, when Doris had pulled into the Burrs' driveway, Emily picked up her purse and got out without saying more than a polite word or two. At home a few minutes later, Doris Schuessler told her husband, "Something is eating at Emily." Despite her devoutness, Emily was also cut off from her church, partly by the same sense of embarrassment that made her hide from her friends, and partly because the minister was a newcomer.

Lone Tree was front-page news that Monday morning, as many of the Burrs' neighbors learned over breakfast. The *Iowa City Press-Citizen* had a feature story about a local science teacher at the Lone Tree High School headlined "Small-Town Living Gets His Vote." Otherwise, it was a quiet morning, even for Lone Tree. "I Love Lucy," "Flipper," and *Wuthering Heights* were on TV, and there were probably fewer than two dozen cars moving in the entire Lone Tree area. Around 10:30 A.M., it began to look like snow, which would prevent Dale from continuing the harvest, but still he lingered. Emily and he had words, as they had often lately. Their conversations were becoming like a waking dream, which always returned to the same horrible point of Emily saying, as she had at the Forbeses', that she did not even have money for groceries.

Right then they were, in fact, nearly out of food, and nearly out of heating oil. Even so, Emily put a package of frozen hamburger on the counter and started a batch of cookies. That was her way, to overcome obstacles by force of niceness and good cooking. Like many Midwestern women, though, she was capable of making niceness carry a variety of emotional messages, and could on occasion be pleasant with a punch. Perhaps she was saying something about Dale's failure as a provider with the slowly thawing hamburger; perhaps she was just doing the only things she knew to help. At any rate, Dale stomped down into the basement. Emily probably thought he was finally going to go out and work, since the Burrs kept their work clothes at the foot of the basement stairs. She could hear him rummaging around, but when he reappeared he had his old Remington model 31 in his hands.

Dale shot Emily at a distance of perhaps ten feet, close enough to char the margins of the wound and tattoo the skin around it with gunpowder. The shot passed through Emily's heart, blowing a gaping hole in her torso, and scattering blood, bits of flesh, pellets, and wadding across the south wall of the kitchen behind her, through an open doorway, and into the living room beyond. Emily clutched the hole in her chest with her right hand as she fell face forward to the floor. Dale stepped over her body lying in the spreading pool of blood, and penned a brief note on a small piece of paper. It said, "John, I'm sorry. I just couldn't stand all the problems." Dale signed it

"Dad," and set it on the counter near his wife's now life-less body.

Then he turned and strode out the back door. His last act of deference to Emily's housecleaning strictures was to wait until he got to his old green and white GMC 4X4 pickup to eject the shell. It was a number-four shot with a red tube, and the last shell in the box. Dale closed the door of the truck and started it up. He let his eyes pass one last time over the place he loved, and then turned around and sped off toward the unsuspecting town.

PART TWO

Ill fares the land, to hastening ills a prey
Where wealth accumulates and men decay.
Oliver Goldsmith

4

Shirley Buline waved at Dale Burr as he drove by in his truck around eleven o'clock. She did not think anything about his not waving back, but she did notice his speed, and the fact that he turned right at the blacktop toward Hills, rather than left toward Lone Tree. "When he turned the corner he really had his foot on it," she said. "He usually didn't drive like that."

Sometime during the ten-minute drive from the Burrs' place to Hills, Dale apparently composed himself and settled on a plan, for he seemed completely at ease once he reached town. He waved at the "boys" inside Hills Grain and Feed as he drove past, and then pulled into the Hills Bank parking lot, where Larry Blake, a Hills Bank cashier, was showing a new employee where to park. Blake, who had known Dale for eight or nine years, waved as the big man in the green coveralls got out of his truck, and Dale reciprocated affably.

Dale went in the back door of the Hills Bank and walked down a short corridor past the empty office of bank president John Hughes. In the main lobby, the cashiers were arrayed on the left under an orange accent stripe. Behind them the bank's vault stood open, allowing entrance to the safe-deposit-box area. To the right were secretaries and potted plants, with the executive offices lining the windows beyond. Dale strode over to the round bank vault door that serves as the bank customers' writing table. A relic of the early days of the Hills Bank, the polished old vault door was intended to remind customers of the bank's antiquity.

To Dale, though, the Hills Bank was a relative newcomer to the Johnson County banking scene. His grandfather's bank in Lone Tree was already sixteen years old when the Hills Bank came into existence in 1907. Before that, local farmers borrowed from institutions in bigger towns like Iowa City. They also relied on individuals, both neighbors and outsiders loaning Eastern capital. No matter how they tried to avoid it, American farmers have almost always had to borrow money to buy land, and often for seed and operating expenses too. Credit has been as crucial as the rain in determining who will succeed and who will fail, and conflict over it has been central to American history since colonial times.

Uproar over the farm debt was, in fact, one of the principal contemporary rationales for the United States Constitution in 1787. In the years immediately after the Revolution, America experienced a profound agricultural depression. Thomas Jefferson noted how "the long succession of years of stunted crops, of reduced prices, the general prostration of the farming business, under levies for the support of manufactures . . . have kept agriculture in a state of abject depression, which has peopled the Western states by silently breaking up those in the Atlantic . . ." Not all debtor farmers were willing to pull up stakes and move on, though.

In the summer of 1786, an armed revolt by indebted farmers broke out in western Massachusetts, an area particularly hard hit by economic distress. During the two years prior to the revolt, 1784–86, the Court of Common Pleas in Hampshire County, Massachusetts, prosecuted 2,977 cases of debt, a 262 percent increase over a two-year period prior to the Revolution. Many of those losing their farms had been Revolutionary soldiers. Returning home after defeating the British, they found their farms in disrepair, their debts swollen, and the price of farm products declining. Scarcely a decade after Valley Forge, Revolutionary War veterans were being evicted from their farms by finance companies, some of which were comprised of European speculators.

Popular outrage over these developments was touched off by a Revolutionary War hero who lost his farm near Pelham, New Hampshire. An eloquent speaker, Daniel Shays captivated audiences in Massachusetts and New Hampshire taverns with discourses on the outrage of good, hard-working men being thrown out of their homes, or worse yet, confined to debtors prison indefinitely, as the law then provided. Shays, who is pictured in a contemporary woodcut as clean shaven and pleasant-featured, would whip the crowd with attacks on the judges and lawyers who figured so prominently in the foreclosure process. Only the rich could hire lawyers, he charged, and as a result they controlled a system that was mercilessly grinding out foreclosures. Shays's solution was breathtakingly simple: "Close down the courts," he exhorted the growing crowds. "Then they can't take our property away or put us in jail."

Even then, contingents led by Shays, Samuel Ely, and others were beginning to forcibly prevent Massachusetts courts, including the State Supreme Court in Springfield, from holding session. Early in 1787, Governor James

Bowdoin sent a force of forty-four hundred men under the command of General Benjamin Lincoln against the insurgents. Shays, who had served with distinction as a captain in the 5th Massachusetts Regiment during the Revolutionary War and once received an ornamental sword from General Lafayette, took command of the much smaller and poorly equipped force of debtor farmers. After unsuccessfully attempting to storm the federal arsenal in Springfield before the arrival of General Lincoln's troops, the small farmers were finally defeated at Petersham on February 7, 1787.

Beaten in the field, the Shayites soon carried the day at the ballot box. In the next elections, most of the legislature that supported Governor Bowdoin was thrown out of office and replaced with staunch small-farm sympathizers. In addition to pardoning Shays and his men, the new legislature enacted laws reducing the cost of court; exempting clothing, household goods, or tools of trade from the debt process; allowing personal property or real estate to be used in payment of loans; and allowing imprisoned debtors to obtain their freedom by taking a debtors' oath. Strong agrarian sentiments were also evident in several other states, such as Rhode Island, which passed a law requiring creditors to accept paper money in payment of debts, and South Carolina and Virginia, where courthouses and poorhouses were burned.

The reason for the overwhelming political success of the Shayites was that the problem they were addressing—the threat of debt to small farmers—was a primary concern to the majority of the people in the United States at the time. As Hector St. John de Crevecoer noted in his 1782 *Letters From an American Farmer,* "Some few towns excepted, we are all tillers of the earth, from Nova Scotia to West Florida. We are a people of cultivators, scattered over an immense territory, communicating with each other by means of good roads and navigable rivers. . . ." The nation's largest city at the time, Philadelphia, had a population of twenty-seven thousand and there were barely fifty thousand people in New York, Boston, and Philadelphia combined at a time when the nation's total population was about three million. There was no way that the centers of banking and commerce could out-vote the agricultural areas.

It was in this atmosphere that the delegates to the Constitutional Convention convened in May 1787. The Annapolis rump convention held the previous spring had been poorly attended, but thanks to the scare that Shays provided, the spring conclave in Philadelphia drew representatives from every state except Rhode Island. Most delegates agreed with Alexander Hamilton that the civil turmoil under the Articles of Confederation was unacceptable and dangerous. Unlike the Shayites, however, they saw the inability to collect debts rather than the inability to pay them as the principal threat to civil peace in the various states. Like a distorted reflection of the actual American populace at the time, the framers of the American Constitution were almost entirely members of the professional, commercial, and banking classes. As Charles A. Beard pointed out in *An Economic Interpretation of the U.S. Constitution,* not a single delegate to the Constitutional Convention was a member of the small-farmer class, which comprised the majority of the country.

In addition, the principal spokesman for small farmers among the American ruling class, Thomas Jefferson, was not just absent from the Constitutional Convention, he was not even in the country. Jefferson was serving as American minister to France during those crucial years of the French

Revolution, and this prevented him from having any direct say in the debate that produced the Constitution. Just as the Constitution of 1787 lacks the lucid, almost poetic style of Jefferson's Declaration of Independence and Virginia Statute of Religious Freedom, it also lacks the sympathy for the yeoman farmer that was at the heart of Jefferson's political philosophy. There were some defenders of the common people at the convention (notably Martin Luther, the delegate from Maryland who refused to sign the document), but most were hostile to their interests.

George Washington, the president of the Constitutional Convention, was a substantial money lender, and had personally suffered losses as a result of agrarian paper-money laws. Washington was also the proprietor of a large progressive farming operation, and an admirer of Sir John Sinclair, a leading ruling-class propagandist for the later English enclosures. On July 20, 1794, Washington wrote to Sinclair that his plan to utterly destroy the commons "must entitle you to [the] warmest thanks" of the English farmer, and farmers around the world, like himself, who read his writings. There is no indication that Washington understood that many of his fellow Americans came to this country to escape the English system and Sinclair's enclosures. Of the two major figures at the convention, Alexander Hamilton openly spit venom at the idea of democracy, and James Madison was hardly any friendlier to the farmers' plight.

The framers of the American Constitution had numerous items on their agenda that fateful summer, including the desire for a uniform currency, security for investment in western lands, and tariff protection for American manufacturers. None was more important, though, than their desire for protection from the paper-money laws, stay laws, pine barrens acts, and other devices for depreciating the currency or delaying the collection of debts that were then emerging with such frequency from the agrarian-controlled state legislatures. They wanted a strong federal government, one with the clear authority to supersede state law in many areas, and the power to suppress uprisings like Shays's Rebellion.

At the same time, the framers of the Constitution sought to insulate the power of government from direct control by the people. This desire is evident throughout the document, from the life appointment of the federal judiciary to the indirect election of the president and senators. Americans today justifiably take great pride in the fact that theirs is the oldest constituted democracy in the world, but to understand American agricultural history, it is important to remember the fundamental hostility of the founding fathers with regard to farmers. As Vernon Louis Parrington noted in his Pulitzer Prize–winning *Main Currents of American Thought,* "It [the Constitution] was the first response to the current liberal demand for written constitutions as a safeguard against tyranny, but it was aimed at the encroachments of agrarian majorities rather than Tory minorities."

Within one year of the ratification of the Constitution by the thirteenth state, the small farmers in western Pennsylvania and neighboring areas had more than a document aimed at them. At Hamilton's urging, Congress voted to assume the states' combined war debts (which the Southern states accepted only after it was agreed that the nation's capital would be located on the Potomac instead of in Philadelphia). Hamilton justified the policy on the grounds of establishing good credit, although opponents charged that many of the notes were by then in the hands of speculators, friends of the treasury secretary, and foreigners. To provide protection and incentives for American industry, Hamilton also planned to shift the tax burden to levies on land, in one form or another.

The Whiskey Tax, which was passed in 1791, was a prime example of this effort, and a cornerstone of Hamilton's program. In it, he tapped a new source of federal revenue by taxing whiskey, the form in which many western farmers moved their corn crop to market in those days of rudimentary bulk transportation. Small farmers howled that Hamilton's program was a baldfaced effort to subsidize the wealthy at the expense of the poor, but the Federalists in Washington were not swayed by such logic. At least forty of the fifty delegates to the Constitutional Convention were holders of securities from the financing of the Revolutionary War. Charles Beard has calculated that repayment of the Revolutionary War debt meant $40 million to such bondholders.

There was popular resistance to the Whiskey Tax from the outset in early 1791, but armed rebellion did not occur until 1794, after Thomas Jefferson had resigned from Washington's Cabinet in protest over the policies of Alexander Hamilton. That summer a delinquent farmer and western Pennsylvania distiller, William Miller, was ordered by a U.S. marshal to leave his farm in the middle of the growing season and appear before a federal judge in Philadelphia. Realizing that the trip to court and the fine would eat up the value of his farm, Miller flew into a rage and attacked the marshal's party.

The revolt spread as quickly as country gossip, and by August 1794 the insurgents held a congress in Parkinson's Ferry to formally begin the process of secession from the union. They occupied Pittsburgh for a time, but proved no match for the fifteen thousand troops called out by President Washington. If Shays's Rebellion had posed the question of whether the United States government was willing to foreclose on Revolutionary War veterans in order to put money in the pockets of speculators, the Whiskey Rebellion answered with a resounding yes.

Then, like so many who came from England and Europe, the exploited small farmer simply moved farther west. The difference was that the English system of industrialization and enclosure was now loose in America. For the next century, the American frontier would be relentlessly pushed forward by two types of men: those who sought America, and those who were running from it.

Dale Burr reached deep within an inside pocket, rummaged awkwardly, and pulled out his checkbook. After writing out a check for five hundred dollars cash, he walked over to the tellers' line. He was wearing heavy soiled green coveralls over a hooded green sweatshirt, blue denim bib overalls, a denim workshirt, green pants with a gold belt buckle, heavy green insulated rubber boots, and waffle-weave long underwear. He might have smelled a little of diesel oil, hog manure, and blood, but no one was offended by the signs of honest toil at the Hills Bank.

While in line, Dale spoke to teller Krista Kirkpatrick, a distant cousin, before stepping to the window of another teller, Denise Maier, around 11:10 A.M. When Dale slid the check across the counter, Maier politely excused herself, indicating she would be right back. Since Dale's name was on a bank "watch list," she asked Roger Reilly, an assistant vice-president, whether it was okay to cash the five-hundred-dollar check. Noting that Dale was already overdrawn about forty-five dollars, Reilly told Maier he would like to talk to him. The teller then returned to her window and asked

Dale to step into Reilly's office, gesturing toward the other side of the bank.

Dale hardly needed any directions to Reilly's window cubicle. He had had several meetings with Reilly over the last few weeks, and two in particular were not the sort a farmer could easily forget. As Dale stepped into his office, Reilly smiled and offered Dale a seat. At age thirty-six, Reilly gave the impression of simultaneously being older and younger than he was, like an aging imp. When he smiled, his upper lip withdrew so that all you saw was teeth. He had been assigned to Dale's account six months earlier when John Hughes, who previously handled the Burr account, foresaw difficulties.

Yet despite distancing himself from Dale Burr, John Hughes maintained total control over his financial affairs. Reilly had very little authority on his own. Dale knew that John Hughes was calling the shots, and it pained him to have been demoted to dealing with an assistant vice-president more than twenty years his junior. Adding embarrassment to the situation was John Hughes's reputation as a famous glad-hander. Hughes was known to interrupt board meetings to take calls from little old ladies, but he had no time anymore to deal with Dale Burr, even though Dale was out almost until midnight the night before trying to harvest beans to pay off loans to his bank.

According to Reilly, "Dale came into my office and presented a check for five hundred dollars payable to Hills Bank and Trust and said he wanted cash for it. I told Dale that he was overdrawn a small amount and went and checked his balance and found that he was overdrawn about forty-five dollars. I told him there was a check in today, a small check, and that he would be overdrawn approximately fifty-five dollars. He said that he was sorry about that but he would take care of it. He pulled out his wallet and gave me sixty dollars—three twenty-dollar bills. I wrote out a deposit ticket and gave him a receipt.

"He talked about going to the FmHA on Tuesday to discuss the loan situation with them. He asked me if I had heard anything from them and I said that we had not." Throughout their conversation, Dale seemed perfectly calm and composed, as if everything had gone as he had expected. Reilly, for his part, seemed relieved that Dale had been able to cover the overdraft on the spot, and apparently did not stop to wonder why Dale would write a check for cash if he had cash in his pocket.

Reilly went to the lavatory after Dale left his office, but Dale did not depart the bank immediately. Once again he lingered. He greeted a couple of people he knew, had a drink at the fountain in the front entryway, and read a couple of the announcements on the bulletin board. Then, as if satisfied, he headed out the door to buy a new box of shotgun shells.

5

It was not unusual to hear John Hughes before you saw him. He liked to wear wingtip shoes with leather heels that clicked when he walked. His cheerful voice often preceded him as well. "Many a time," recounted Ruth Forbes, "I'd be in the bank and he would shout from behind his desk, 'So how are the Forbeses today, and tell me about those boys of yours.' 'Helloooo,' he'd say, 'helloooo.' "

Physically, John Hughes was not the sort of person you would pick to be on your basketball team. Even though at six feet one inch he was a shade taller than Dale Burr, the Hills Bank president was not an athletic-looking guy. "He did not have what you would call an hourglass build," recalled a friend. "He had skinny legs and was kind of big in the torso." His clean-cut face was handsome, though, and illuminated by the boyish gap-tooth grin that was his trademark.

Perpetually upbeat, John Hughes seemed to genuinely relish the chitchat about the weather and local sports that makes up so much polite Iowa small talk. An enthusiastic sports fan, he was particularly devoted to the Chicago Cubs in baseball, and the University of Iowa in football. Although he attended both the University of Iowa and Iowa State University, he remained unswervingly loyal to the U of I Hawkeyes. Once when he was an undergraduate at Iowa State, he was discovered at home watching the Hawkeye game on TV instead of out at the stadium watching the (Iowa State) Cyclones. As punishment, someone directed his fraternity pledge class to throw him in the shower.

Iowa City attorney Robert Downer, who was one year ahead of Hughes in the University of Iowa law school, remembers first noticing John Hughes's comments about the Cubs. "I liked John initially because of the commitment that he showed to an organization in which he believed," he said. As he got to know John Hughes better, Downer came to realize that he was not only loyal, but also surprisingly open-minded. Neither then as a law-school student nor later as a bank officer was he a snob. He would socialize with almost anyone, and he had friends from all walks of life. His mind was quick and disciplined, and he was particularly attracted to people with dynamic capabilities. Friends say this is why Hughes strongly supported Iowa Congressman Jim Leach, who was politically more liberal than Hughes himself.

John Hughes grew up on a farm six miles northwest of Hills during the Forties and Fifties. His father, Cecil Hughes, was a pure-bred Duroc hog man. Everette Winborn, Hughes's childhood 4-H leader, recalls, "He was a jolly, outgoing kid. I don't think he ever made trouble in 4-H. He was up front, a model kid." Like Vernon Burr and many of the more able, ambitious children from farm families in the area, he attended high school in Iowa City, graduating in 1957. That fall, he enrolled at Iowa State University in Ames, where he began majoring in agriculture, but switched to industrial administration. A good student, Hughes went from there straight to law school at the University of Iowa in Iowa City.

Five years of practicing law in nearby Cedar Rapids followed. While he was getting his feet on the ground in the legal profession, he met a young schoolteacher who made quite an impression on him. She too had recently graduated from a major Midwestern university, and like so many of the people to whom John Hughes was drawn, she was bright and dynamic. John Hughes wooed his future wife, Karen, to Cedar Rapids. It was also here that their oldest daughter, Emily, was born. Then in 1969 he was hired at his hometown bank, the Hills Bank and Trust Company. Although he started as a junior officer, the Hills Bank job proved to be the opportunity of a lifetime for John Hughes.

Founded in January 1907 by John A. Goetz, a former associate of Dale Burr's grandfather at the Lone Tree Bank, the Hills Bank grew because of astute management. It was one of the few rural Iowa banks that never closed its doors during the Great Depression. Then, after World War II, when the Lone Tree Bank and others were inclined to keep a tight rein on credit, Albert Droll, the president of the Hills Bank, took a much more liberal tack. One retired farmer recalled how in the late 1940s "Albert Droll said he would loan forty thousand dollars to any farmer who owned his farm. At the time, this was thought to be a scandalously reckless thing to do, but of course the inflation in land values covered the loans many times over."

The Hills Bank attracted considerable new business as a result of Droll's approach, and it kept almost all of it. The people at the Hills Bank were known for their politeness and consideration. During the 1960s, the Hills Bank grew to the point of putting real pressure on some of its competitors. By 1971, the once lordly Lone Tree Bank's position had become so weak that the board of directors, among them Vernon Burr, decided to merge it with the other bank in town, the Farmers and Merchants Bank. The Burrs did all right financially on the deal, but the decision was an important one for the community and the family both. More than just the disappearance of the old Lone Tree Bank name, it meant the end of the Burrs' direct management ties to the bank in town.

Meanwhile over at the Hills Bank, it was already apparent that Albert Droll had found what country folk call a "gooder" in John Hughes. "John was a perfectionist, and banking was his dream," said one close business associate, who described him as a "workaholic" who would frequently put in sixteen-hour days and could often be found at the bank on Sundays after church. Willis Bywater, a former high-school classmate whom Hughes brought onto the bank's board of directors, said Hughes's concern for his customers was legendary. If he was in the bank after hours, he insisted on answering the telephone personally, even though a recorded message with the bank's hours was available. "He was never too busy to pick up the phone and talk to someone," Bywater said, adding that he had even seen Hughes interrupt board of directors meetings to talk with a customer.

Karen Hughes said, "At the office, his calls were seldom screened. People could call him straight, and many, many people did. He also got calls at home at all hours of day and night. He believed in people. He was a farmer too. Did you know that?" she asked. "He always thought of himself as a farmer. He'd get down in the hog yards and walk with the farmers. He could do that because he was one of them." At the same time, John Hughes was unsurpassed at observing the social niceties. He sent congratulatory notes to bank customers when mention of their family appeared in the newspaper, and he was known to attend a half-dozen weddings and funerals during a weekend.

When Albert Droll died in 1975, John Hughes was named to succeed him as president of the bank. Although Hughes's youth (he was then thirty-six) surprised some, it was an astute choice on the part of the Hills board. No one could match John Hughes's mixture of legal training and farm-boy savvy. There was also something about John Hughes that transcended the numbers. In the boardroom of the Hills Bank, he put up a small poster with one word on it: "Quality." In a direct and personal way, Hughes strove to make this a central tenet of the Hills Bank. "He made you feel good," recalled one associate. "He was always very positive, and had a way of coming up with concrete solutions to problems."

It was John Hughes's idea, for instance, to move the Hills Bank into the lucrative suburban and urban Iowa City market, which proved the foundation of its prosperity during the late 1970s and early 1980s. He also showed uncommonly good judgment in the people to whom he extended credit. As Robert Downer noted, "People in town went down to [the Hills Bank] to borrow money, and they turned out to be some of the most successful people in the area." In 1975, Hills Bank had assets of $36.4 million and deposits of $33.2 million. At the end of Hughes's first decade at the bank's helm, assets were $219.8 million and deposits were $199.7 million. "You have to give John credit," said Harold Schuessler, a member of the Hills Bank board and Dale Burr's close neighbor to the east. "John knew all the angles. When an opportunity presented itself, he was ready to move on it."

A prime example of John Hughes's acuity was the Hills railroad right-of-way annexation he helped engineer during the late 1970s and early 1980s. Under Iowa law, a bank from one town cannot open an office in another town where there is already a bank, unless the two towns are "contiguous." Since eight miles separated Hills from Iowa City, the Hills Bank could not open a branch in the much larger neighboring community, even though more than 40 percent of its deposits came from there. "I think our banking laws as they pertain to branches make absolutely no sense," said Hughes, who confided to the *Des Moines Register* that he had long been looking for a way into Iowa City. The bank could have asked state banking authorities for permission to move its headquarters to Iowa City, but Hughes decided it was more important to the personality of the bank to keep the headquarters in Hills, "Where Town and Country Meet."

Then, in 1979, John Hughes was approached by childhood friends Ron and Jim Stutsman, co-owners of Stutsman's Farm Supply. Curiously, the Stutsmans came in asking about a loan for the Rock Island Railroad, which operated the spur line from Hills to Iowa City. It soon became apparent that the Stutsmans' business was itself in some financial difficulty, though. They had recently invested a good deal of money expanding their fertilizer business without getting more than an oral commitment from the Rock Island that it would maintain service to the Hills spur. Now, a few months later, the financially strapped railroad had changed its mind. "Rock Island apparently told Stutsman's that they wouldn't ship any more railroad cars unless they got a hundred-thousand-dollar interest-free loan from Stutsman's, or from somebody, that they could then repay by granting credit on the number of cars ordered," said Hills Bank officer Jim Gordon.

It looked like another small blow to another small town, but in this problem for Stutsman's Farm Supply, John Hughes saw the glimmer of something grand. He said he was not interested in loaning money to Rock Island, but he might be able to help. Hughes initiated discussions with people like Hills City Attorney Jay Honohan and Cedar Rapids and Iowa City Railroad (CRANDIC) president Otis Woods, which led to the formulation of a concrete plan. The idea was that first the City of Hills would annex the old Rock Island right-of-way. This would enable Hills to issue industrial revenue bonds to subsidize the railroad, and would also give Hills a hundred feet of contiguous boundary with Iowa City. The bonds were supposed to sweeten the deal by helping finance the purchase of the spur from the now-bankrupt Rock Island Line by CRANDIC, and possibly help restore the tracks and bridge over the Iowa River. The Hills Bank, for its part, pledged to purchase the bonds if no other buyer could be found.

The scheme was publicly championed by Larry Culver, who was both Stutsman's accountant and the mayor of Hills. In a typically small-town manner (a record of town business was sometimes "published" by taping the minutes of town meetings to the door at City Hall), the City of Hills first sought permission from the state to annex the railroad right-of-way all the way into Iowa City on the grounds that it was needed to save a local family-owned, farm-related business. Then it authorized issuance of up to $672,000 in industrial bonds to entice CRANDIC to purchase the spur from the federally appointed bankruptcy trustee for the Rock Island. Since these industrial revenue bonds were backed by the tax revenues of the town of Hills, the people of Hills were ultimately behind the whole deal, from the acquisition of the property to the railroad subsidy to the Hills Bank's commission on the bond issue.

John Hughes and the Hills Bank maintained a relatively low profile throughout the dicey and seemingly endless negotiations necessary to bring the deal to culmination. The bank was aided in this effort by the fact that the local newspaper, the *Iowa City Press-Citizen,* carried almost nothing on the matter. The Iowa City bureau of the *Cedar Rapids Gazette* ran a dozen or so pieces, but they treated the annexation issue as an embattled small-town farm business story. The public was given no clue that the railroad right-of-way annexation being promoted by Stutsman's would allow the Hills Bank into Iowa City, let alone that this might be the driving economic force behind the project. This vital connection was not revealed until after the state board had approved Hills's annexation proposal, and even then the story was broken by a paper 125 miles away, the *Des Moines Register.*

Although Hughes characterized benefits to the bank from the annexation deal as "a side effect," it was actually quite a significant matter, as evidenced by the fact that the $672,000 the bank pledged to the purchase of the utility bonds was almost exactly the institution's legal lending limit at the time. John Hughes was willing to shoot the limit because the deal promised to make the bank money in numerous ways. In the first place, it gave him the face interest on the loan, which was secured in granite by governmental pledge. Beyond that, it buttressed other investments and loans and maintained the viability of the Hills Bank's investment in the main Hills businesses. These factors alone would probably be enough to persuade most bankers to underwrite such a bond issue, but they were actually just minor sidelights for the Hills Bank and John Hughes.

When the various portions of the deal were finally sealed, the City of Hills acquired a ward eight miles long and one hundred feet wide, Stutsman's maintained railroad service to its mill, CRANDIC got its new publicly subsidized spur line, and John Hughes had his opening into Iowa City. All parties appeared pleased, but for Hughes especially it was a masterful deal, carried out so smoothly that Iowa City did not catch on until it was too late. Soon the Hills Bank was pushing other deals which gave the bank the extra security of a mortgage on the public tax revenues of the community, rather than a mortgage on the object of the loan.

In a way, this was typical of John Hughes's loan policies. While his predecessor, Albert Droll, would extend small loans to members of old families in the area on the basis of their good name, Hughes was not interested in making unsecured loans. One Hills area farmer remembers going to John Hughes for a small nonagricultural loan around 1980. "I'd been banking at the Hills Bank for thirty years nearly," he said, "ever since I was tall enough to shove the money over the counter to the teller. And I'd done a fair amount of business with them over that time. Well, one day I went in and applied for a thousand-dollar loan. John Hughes called me in and asked me what I wanted the money for." The farmer, who came from an old and prominent family around Hills, said he was kind of worn down. He wanted to take a little Mexican vacation.

Hughes inquired, "What have you got for collateral?"

"Collateral, hell," the hog farmer later snorted. "The guy before'd let you borrow on your signature. So I said, 'I got a horse.'"

"He said, 'I don't ride horses.'

"I said, 'I got a motorcycle.'

"He said, 'I don't ride motorcycles.' "

Finally, Hughes told the farmer he could have the loan if he wanted to pledge some real estate. The farmer said he could have given the bank a mortgage on any of the four houses he owned, "but I'd already decided that if I couldn't do it on personal credit, I wasn't going to do it. So I told him, 'No, thanks.' "

With agricultural loans, Hughes was similarly inclined to protect himself. Often, his cleverness and up-to-the-minute understanding of legal and financial developments made it possible for him to offer farmers attractive deals, but he never did so on what they call a "guts and hide" basis (where the loan takes guts and everybody stands to lose their hide). In fact, despite the bank's ubiquitous calendars proclaiming it "Iowa's largest rural bank," the Hills Bank actually held a relatively small portfolio of agricultural loans.

Hills Bank attorney Downer said that under Hughes's direction "the bank was never one to throw caution to the wind with farm borrowers. . . . John was concerned that on the long-term basis farmers were buying land at prices that wouldn't cash-flow. He was concerned about farmers with high net worth but poor profitability. He could see that farmers were buying land that, even with good [crop] prices, would never pay. He felt this simply could not continue."

It turned out that John Hughes was correct in this judgment, and so once again the Hills Bank caught the turn of the financial tide before most of the competition. Just as Albert Droll was one of the first to loosen the reins of farm credit in Johnson County during the 1950s,

John Hughes was one of the first to tighten down during the 1980s.

Between them, Hughes and Droll represented the two sides of the farm-financing coin. For nearly two hundred years, the ebb and flow of farm credit and the accompanying phenomenon of boom and bust have been so essential to the American experience that the two antipodes have almost seemed to blend together.

Charles Dickens wrote of a visit to America during the 1840s: "If its individual citizens, to a man, are to be believed, it always is depressed, and always is stagnated, and always is at an alarming crisis, and never was otherwise; though as a body they are ready to make an oath on the evangelists at any hour of the day or night, that it is the most prosperous of all countries on the habitable globe."

In fact, of course, boom and bust have been quite distinct, and their repeated occurrence in American agriculture provides one of the most regular cycles in our economic history. During the nineteenth century, for instance, five major agricultural credit crises occurred at roughly twenty-year intervals. Regardless of war, the political party in office, or religious fervor, the cycle repeated, reshaping ownership of the American landscape much as repeated freezing and thawing reshapes the surface of the farmer's fields.

The first great American crash of the nineteenth century occurred in 1819, when the widespread collapse in the credit purchase of Western lands produced a major national depression. The immediate trigger of the Panic of 1819 was the collapse of the Second Bank of the United States, which had been recklessly managed, but ironically the process of economic upheaval ultimately increased bank control of

Western real estate. In the wake of large numbers of state bank failures, vast areas of the West became the property of the First Bank of the United States, commonly vituperated by Western farmers as "The Monster."

Congress did away with credit sales of land altogether after the crash. Public land sales slumped badly, and economic depression gripped the country until 1822. Among the factors that contributed to the recovery of American agriculture—which is to say the American economy in the days when farmers constituted nearly 70 percent of the nation's work force—were the invention of a cast-iron sheathed plow, which was patented in 1819 by Jethro Wood, and the continued influx of immigrants. Good land, good farmers, and good machinery made possible tremendous increases in virtually every area of American farm production during the early decades of the nineteenth century.

Then, in 1837, it all came crashing down again. Land speculation, much of it by banks and bankers, was again the underlying cause of the panic. Among the prominent plungers was the brother of Andrew Jackson's attorney general, who was part of a syndicate that used money from the New York Life Insurance Company and several banks with which its members were associated to buy a third of a million acres in eight states and territories. President Andrew Jackson might denounce land speculation, but there was really little fundamental ideological disagreement between the two parties on this point. As Theodore Parker, the prominent Boston clergyman, noted: "The Whig inaugurates Money got; the Democrat inaugurates the Desire to get money."

The Panic of 1837 was triggered by President Jackson's order to accept only silver for purchase of federal land after August 11, 1837. Jackson's aim was to reduce Western land speculation, but the medicine proved stronger than he expected and, with his veto of the rechartering of Hamilton's National Bank, provoked a total financial collapse. In late April, one observer on Wall Street noted sourly that "the whole city [meaning New York] is going to the devil from a pecuniary point of view. . . ." The effect of the panic was, if anything, even greater out West, especially Iowa. The first land office to process sales of the Black Hawk Purchase was not opened until June 1838, at which point there were already twenty-three thousand settlers on the Iowa prairie from Lone Tree to Burr Oak who were technically trespassers.

The squatters clung fiercely to their land, developing the so-called "claim clubs" to protest their homesteads. When a section was put on the block, claim club members would go en masse to the sale and physically prevent anyone from contesting the claim of the homesteader, or bidding above the minimum price. Johnson County, Iowa, developed what has been called "one of the most perfect" claim clubs in all Iowa, but even so the majority of squatters in the Black Hawk Purchase were fighting a losing battle. Payments on loans (which frequently carried interest rates of 30 percent and higher) were delayed and then suspended. Many farmers gave it up, and joined those moving farther west.

Bitterness over usury was responsible for the hostility the new state showed toward banks in its early years. Most of the delegates to Iowa's first constitutional convention were Jacksonian Democrats who cheered when speaker Jonathan Hall declared that "a Bank of earth is the best Bank, and the best share is the Plow share." After the repeal of the Bank of Dubuque's charter in 1845, banks were banned outright in the state for thirteen years. During this period, Iowa resorted to many expedients to transact the business of society, including hundreds of different types of notes issued by banks outside the state and six kinds of local "script of orders." Almost all of this currency circulated below par, and was subject to wild gyrations in value.

In Iowa, popular reaction against this sort of financial chaos was as great as the reaction against bankers had been in the first place. Prosperity returned again to American agriculture during the 1840s, taking much the shape it had the previous two times through the cycle. Kicked off by new developments in agricultural technology (such as John Deere's 1837 one-piece plow made of saw-steel that was able to cut the virgin prairie sod), and reinforced with new immigrants (such as the Burrs), the wave rose again. By the mid-1840s, Western land speculation was again robust enough to amaze Dickens. "The more absurd the project, the more remote the object, the more madly they are pursued," he wrote. "Not the puniest brook on the shore of Lake Michigan was suffered to remain without a city at its mouth."

The next crash came exactly twenty years after its predecessor. Caused by speculation in railroads and real estate, the Panic of 1857 was violent but brief. Thousands of farmers and businesses went bankrupt, and banks throughout the country were forced to suspend specie payments for a period. The fledgling Republican Party reaped considerable political advantage from the crash, especially in Iowa, where the voters returned Republican majorities in both houses of the legislature, as well as a Republican governor and two Republican congressmen. Seizing the opportunity, the Republicans convened a new constitutional convention to rewrite the fundamental law of the state.

These newly empowered Republicans were both abolitionists and ambitious capitalists, desiring to remove the shackles from banks as well as blacks. More than a passing political fancy, the Republicans' rise to power reflected a basic political realignment occurring among farmers all over the country. The Jacksonian Democrats' alliance of Western and Southern agricultural interests against Northern commerce was giving way to more purely regional alliances of North against South. Frustrated by the South's blockage of federal programs to benefit free farmers, and agitated to the edge of violence by the experiences of John Brown and Bloody Kansas, Iowa farmers felt little sympathy for their Southern counterparts.

The South, for its part, was increasingly disinclined to apologize for its "peculiar institution." In the early years under the Constitution, Southerners generally assumed that slavery would wither with the development of the country, but new advances in agricultural technology powered a rise in human bondage. After 1793, Yale graduate Eli Whitney's cotton gin, which mechanically removed the seeds from the boll, quickly transformed cotton into a practical crop for slave agriculture. Thereafter, cotton production and the synonymous social condition of slavery dramatically turned the tide of history in the South. Between 1840 and 1860, Southern cotton production tripled, and the slave population increased from 2.4 million to 3.8 million blacks.

No lengthy study was needed to convince free Northern farmers that slave agriculture represented a tremendous threat to them. On the one hand, they knew that to compete side-by-side with slave agriculture they would have to literally work themselves like slaves. Slavery thus represented an immediate reduction in the economic value of their labor. Beyond that, the free farmers of the North became increasingly chilled by the political effects of slavery, and the suggestion that human bondage might be the future of all American agriculture. Certainly spokesmen for the vainglorious Southern planter aristocracy made no effort to hide their contempt for all who actually worked the land with their hands. "The laboring population of no nation on earth are entitled to liberty," declared one South Carolinian, "or capable of enjoying it."

At the outset of the Civil War, Southern agriculture was characterized by large-scale commercial farming of cotton with slave labor, while Northern agriculture was character- ized by smaller, diversified free family farms. Although the commercial value of the former exceeded the latter when the guns sounded at Fort Sumter, the latter proved much more resilient during the intense test that followed. Once again, as in early England, the yeomen proved the strength of the nation, besting their Southern counterparts with rifle and plow both. Despite the absence of a million agricultural workers during the Civil War, Northern agricultural pro- duction actually increased, while Southern agriculture with- ered in the stranglehold of the Northern blockade.

The key to the Northern farmer's success was the most intensive mechanization yet witnessed in American agricul- ture. "Machinery and improved implements have been em- ployed to a much greater extent during the years of rebellion than ever before," noted the Ohio State Board of Agricul- ture in 1863, adding that "without drills, corn-planters, reapers and mowers, horse-rakes, hay elevators, and thresh- ing machines, it would have been impossible to have seeded and gathered the crops of 1863 . . ." That same year Iowa farmers harvested 63.8 million bushels of corn (for an aver- age of 36 bushels per acre), and the Iowa State Agricultural Society declared that "corn is the principal element of our wealth."

Despite the war, the 1860s were relatively good years for free farmers in America. As a reward for farmers' support of President Abraham Lincoln and the Republicans in the

1860 election, Congress passed four major agricultural reform acts that had been blocked by the South: the Homestead Act, the Morrill Land Grant College Act, the Transcontinental Railroad Act, and the bill establishing the Department of Agriculture. The last was perhaps the most important, for even though agriculture was "admittedly the largest interest in the nation," as Lincoln put it, the farmers' interests had been served only by a clerkship.

The Union government's inflation of currency through the issuance of paper money to fund the war also helped farmers by making it easier for them to pay off their debts. The reversal of Northern farmers' fortunes really began with Appomattox. Freed to return to civilian life, Civil War veterans helped precipitate a serious decline in agricultural prices. Farmers who had borrowed money to expand or acquire the new machinery now found themselves in a tightening vise. Many were in financial difficulty from 1870 on, but it was not until 1873 that thousands of Northern farmers began to pay for the Union victory with the foreclosure of their farms.

The next crash in the cycle, the Panic of 1873, was caused by wild speculation in virtually every aspect of the economy, especially railroads. Presaged by the Credit Mobilier scandal of 1872, the panic was actually triggered by tightening credit, represented most prominently by the Fourth Coinage Act. Passed by Congress and signed by President Ulysses S. Grant in February 1873, the act demonetarized silver and put the nation exclusively on a gold standard. Although little understood at the time of its adoption (a year later Grant himself wrote to a correspondent complaining of the insufficient supply of silver dollars, apparently not realizing that the demonetarization of silver meant no more silver coins), the act became the focus of American political debate during the last quarter of the nineteenth century.

Farmers spoke quaintly of "too much hog in the dollar," but beneath the colloquialism their economic intelligence was keen. The effect of the Coinage Act of 1873 was to make money dearer, with the result that commodities like hogs were worth less, and debts were more difficult to repay. Then, in January 1875, Congress passed the Specie Resumption Act, which provided for the resumption of specie payments, and significantly reduced the amount of paper money in circulation, thus bringing Civil War financing to an end. With both silver and paper currency reduced, the country was thrown into a drastic deflation. In ten years the money circulation was reduced from somewhat more than $2.1 billion to a little over a billion, or from $58 per capita to $17 per capita. Gold might remain stable, but somehow "them steers," as one observer quipped, "while they grew well, shrank in value as fast as they grew."

The farmers' initial response was to organize, giving rise to the Patrons of Husbandry, better known as the Grange. Founded by Oliver Kelley of Minnesota in 1867, the Grange lobbied hard for public control of the railroads, resulting in a wave of "Granger laws" which attempted to dictate railroad rates at the state level. By 1873, there were more than two thousand Grange chapters in Iowa alone, but the subsequent prosperity made Iowa farmers inclined to seek technological rather than political solutions to their problems. Barn architecture was then the focus of considerable thought, and so beginning in the 1880s, Iowa farmers built hundreds of eight-sided and round barns. These structures contained more storage space than rectangular barns of the same height, and were further favored for their shorter distances between feed and animals, a crucial consideration in an age when virtually all work inside the barn was still done by hand.

Iowa also boasted the most complete railroad system in the country by 1880, with 5,235 miles of track and no resident farther than twenty-five miles from a railroad station. This greatly altered the economic horizon of the Midwestern farmer, for his market was no longer thirty miles away, but three thousand miles away. Growth for export had become a significant part of the American grain farmer's business by the 1870s, and it continued to grow as frenzied railroad expansion throughout the West dramatically expanded the nation's agricultural acreage. With corn and wheat rolling off the American plains in ever greater quantities, the American farmer took the world food trade by storm. Blessed with low overhead and virgin soil—and lacking major competition—he could effectively set the world price for his crops for a time during the latter nineteenth century.

Not all American farmers shared in the prosperity, though. Farmers in older, more established areas such as New England found that they could not compete with the low prices of produce coming off the plains any more than could foreign farmers. Often too small or too hilly to employ the latest machinery, these farms were squeezed tighter and tighter while their owners, like the farmer in William Dean Howells's *The Landlord at Lion's Head,* dreamed of getting out and starting over in "Californy." Thousands of these Eastern farms were abandoned during the later part of the century, as witnessed by the stone fences commonly found snaking through the middle of hundred-year-old woods in New England today.

Falling exactly twenty years after its predecessor, the Crash of 1893 bankrupted an estimated six hundred banks, fifteen thousand businesses, and one-third of the nation's railroads. Although unemployment was widespread, many more farmers were forced to leave the land and seek jobs in the towns and cities. The causes of the Crash of 1893 were familiar (with railroads again playing a particularly large part), but the effects were worse, according to railroad magnate James J. Hill, because "everything is built up" and the nation was "no longer a frontier country." Hill predicted the date of the crash within a few days of when it actually occurred. At that time, according to his son, "he had nothing in his box. As he said, 'not a pound of meal.' He had only cash. He had sold everything in the Great Northern and Northern Pacific. Perhaps he had fifty million."

Meanwhile in the American heartland, thousands of farmers had nothing but meal. Historian Vernon Louis Parrington has written how, after the crash when his father was about to lose his Kansas farm because there was no market and his crop was worthless, the family sat around the stove listening as the big full ears of corn "burned briskly, popping and crackling in the jolliest fashion. And if while we sat around such a fire watching the year's crop go up the chimney, the talk sometimes became bitter about railroads and middlemen, who will wonder? We were in a fitting mood to respond to Mary Ellen Lease and her doctrine of raising less corn and more hell."

Concluding that "plutocracy has . . . been enthroned upon the ruins of democracy," a grass-roots movement of practical, straightforward farmers set out to reclaim America from a century of increasing corruption. The man the populists rallied around as their standard bearer was William Jennings Bryan, the "boy orator of the Platte." Bryan won the Democratic Party's presidential nomination with a ringing defense of the small farmer and the silver dollar. "We shall answer their demands for a gold standard by saying to them, 'You shall not press down upon the brow of labor this crown of thorns,' " Bryan declared. " 'You shall not crucify mankind upon a cross of gold.' "

On the face of it, it might seem that Bryan held the high ground over his Republican opponent, William McKinley. Not only had McKinley sponsored the tariff act that helped trigger the Panic of '93, but farmers still constituted a popular majority in America in 1896. As always, however, they were deeply divided. Southern farmers still largely refused to join hands with their Northern counterparts, and Northern farmers were themselves hardly of one mind. A multitude of cultural and religious differences split them, as did conflicting political aspirations.

Bryan's campaign ultimately foundered in places like Iowa, where staunch Republican farmers like the Burrs gave the "great commoner" fewer votes than any Democrat since Hancock in 1880. Although Bryan called it "the first battle," the presidential campaign of 1896 was in fact the last battle of agrarian America. Never again would a major American political party make agrarian issues its central concern.

6

The door to the Hills barbershop jangled as Dale Burr pushed it open. Inside he was greeted by Dennis Busch, the proprietor. Busch had an empty chair, but Dale had not come for a haircut.

Like many in the Midwest, the Hills barbershop did a brisk side business in ammunition, primarily for bird hunting. The ammo brought the men into the store, got them spending money, and helped perpetuate the ancient manly ritual of the barbershop.

Busch, a well-groomed man in his mid-thirties, normally sold Dale Burr one box of shotgun shells a year. Now that pheasant-hunting season was under way, it appeared that this was what Dale had in mind. "I've got a nephew who's going hunting and needs a box of ammo," he said, adding that he wanted 12-gauge shells. Busch offered either number-four or number-six shot.

After a moment's consideration, Dale took the heavier number-four shot. These shells are good for long-distance hunting. Experienced pheasant hunters often load number-four shot as the second or third shell in the magazine so that they can still try for a fleeing bird if their first shot misses. The drawback of number-four shot is that if you hit something at close range it can tear it up pretty badly.

It was a little before 11:30 A.M. when Dale left Busch's Barber Shop with his shotgun shells. He got into his pickup and drove west down Hills's main street. Once out of the barber's sight, Dale doubled back around the Hills Bank again and into the parking lot. Opening the new-smelling box of shells, he filled the magazine of his Remington model-31 shotgun with a practiced hand. Then he unzipped his full-length coveralls and ran the barrel of the gun down the leg into his boot. After swinging out of the cab of his truck, he walked toward the back door of the Hills Bank again, where he could see John Hughes working in his office.

Hughes had, in fact, just arrived at the bank, having spent the morning of December 9 in Iowa City attending to a number of small errands. Early Monday he kept a regular appointment at University Hospital in Iowa City, where he received an ultraviolet-ray treatment for the chronic dermatosis on his legs, torso, and arm. In typical fashion, Hughes teased Mary Lou Fairchild, the physical therapist, about getting tickets to watch the Hawkeye football team play in the Rose Bowl, which was then still nearly a month away. "We kidded each other a lot about the Hawks," she said. "He always brightened up everybody's day. He was one of the cheeriest, nicest people."

The next stop for John Hughes was across town at Mary L. Kelly's funeral. The Kellys were old friends of the Hugheses, and Mary Kelly's son, Cork, was personally close to John Hughes. The elder Kelly had founded Protein

Blenders, a feed operation in Iowa City. After his death in the early 1960s, however, the firm fell on hard times. Mismanagement caused every bank in Iowa City to refuse to loan money to the company. At one point, the Hills Bank was the only one that would lend money to Protein Blenders. Later, when the firm rebounded to become a major Iowa City farm industry under Cork Kelly's leadership, it remained loyal to the Hills Bank.

John Hughes drove from the University of Iowa medical complex across the Iowa River to the funeral at St. Patrick's Catholic Church. Parking nearby, he walked across the frozen snow to the arched entryway. Afterward, he talked to several people he knew. Then he headed for work, tucking the funeral announcement in his left inside coat pocket as he departed. Back behind the wheel of his new blue Oldsmobile, he drove south from Iowa City toward Hills. He had a very full schedule ahead of him, and to the extent that his thoughts wandered, they likely turned to his two daughters, Emily and Amy.

Dark-haired Emily, seventeen, was already a real beauty, while Amy, fourteen, was just beginning to come into her own as a young woman. John adored them both and loved spending time with them, especially over the chess board. He was involved in several of Emily and Amy's church and school activities, but sometimes he wished he could do more. One of the unavoidable side effects of his heavy business and social schedule was that he sometimes had less time for his family than for his community. Recently, friends had begun to tell John they frankly thought he should devote more time to his kids.

"John Hughes was a workaholic," said a Hills Bank board member. "He didn't see enough of his children. He didn't see his kids play basketball. I told him, 'You know, they're only kids once.' " The Hills Bank, and especially certain members of the bank's board of directors, were like family to John Hughes too, and so he took their advice seriously. This was one reason that he had just turned down an offer to head the Iowa State Bankers' Association. Ordinarily, the presidency of the bankers association was something he would have jumped at. In 1985, though, he respectfully declined, explaining to friends that he wanted to spend more time with the girls.

The twelve-mile drive from Iowa City to Hills took about twenty minutes, putting him in his office in Hills about the time that Dale finally left the bank after his meeting with Roger Reilly about the overdraft. As soon as he arrived, John Hughes wanted some information on clients. Comptroller James Pratt brought a group of files into the bank president's office and sat down in a chair between the desk and the window. Just then the phone rang, and Hughes, plastic coffee cup in hand, turned away. Anymore, as Iowans say, it seemed that the phone was always ringing for John Hughes.

Out-of-state banks sought him out as a consultant with increasing frequency, and his local financial horizon had widened dramatically as well. By the mid-1980s, Hughes's primary interests were directed toward financing construction, transportation, and even the commercialization of University of Iowa research, as much as farming. His great enthusiasm of the moment was the First Capital Development Corporation, a joint venture of the Chamber of Commerce, the City of Iowa City, and the University of Iowa, which was designed to develop commercial applications of University of Iowa discoveries, such as Bufferin and Pepsodent.

Like the institution he headed, John Hughes's rapid personal rise owed a great deal to the amazing dividends the

Hills railroad annexation deal had paid. In November 1982, when the Hills Bank opened its lavish new Iowa City branch, John Hughes gave the bank's assets as $102 million and deposits as $92 million. Three years later, the bank had doubled both figures, adding as much growth in thirty-six months as it had in its previous seventy-five years. The fact that the period was the worst financially for Iowa bankers in nearly fifty years further enhanced Hughes's reputation, for as Andrew Carnegie noted a century before, "The man who has money during a panic is the wise and valuable citizen."

By the mid-1980s John Hughes had become the most successful person ever to emerge from Hills, with the possible exception of Louis Jenn, the founder of Jenn-Aire Corporation, the Indianapolis-based manufacturer of stoves and ovens. Although no one else in his family was in banking, a number were leaders in their own fields. One brother, Gary Hughes, was Johnson County Sheriff, while the other brother, Jim Hughes, was regional vice-president of Equitable Life in Des Moines. Even his young sister Carolyn, who was married to a Hills area farmer, had distinguished herself as a leader of the Iowa City Parent Teacher Organization. Among other prominent Hugheses were one cousin who was on the County Board of Supervisors, and another cousin who was head of the State Bar Association.

John Hughes had some enemies, but mostly the people of Hills looked on him with a sort of proprietary pride. He was generally well-liked, and definitely thought of as a local boy, even though he (like most of the Hills Bank's management) actually lived in Iowa City. The locals were impressed that John Hughes had done it all in Hills, before their very eyes, so to speak. And if there was some realization that the citizens of Hills had gotten the least from the railroad annexation scheme done in their name, most people relished the genius of what Hughes had wrought. "Quite a deal," a longtime Hills area resident commented on the affair. "Quite a deal."

Another reason people appreciated John Hughes was his almost superhuman involvement with charitable and fraternal organizations. In addition to work with St. Andrew's Presbyterian Church (for which he arranged a sizable loan at a favorable rate of interest), he was active in support of the Masonic Order, Iowa City Mercy Hospital, Hawkeye Swim Club, Iowa City Chamber of Commerce, Iowa City Rotary Club, and Hills Community Club, as well as fundraising for numerous University of Iowa causes. In addition, he was tabbed by the Iowa State Bankers Association to serve on a committee to draft recommendations on the most emotionally explosive subject facing the banking community, namely farm debt. Hughes's report on the farm finance crisis was praised for its even-handedness and compassion for the farmer.

As much as Hughes himself made new agricultural loans, though, he liked the deals to be blue chip. The Hills Bank actually had more leeway than many other banks because of its profitability, but Hughes insisted the bank not carry losers. "He was especially concerned about making sure that the bank was extremely sound," said Iowa City attorney Robert Downer. And as always, he insisted on very comfortable collateral backing. Clearly, this is what he thought he had gotten into with Dale Burr. Having grown up on a farm in the vicinity of Hills, he knew the Burrs' reputation as able, land-rich farmers who had built one of the largest operations in the area over five generations. On March 10, 1984, when he extended his first large loan to Dale, John Hughes noted in the Hills Bank ledger on the Burr account that Dale owed the Hills Bank $360,000, against collateral of 246 acres "conservatively" valued at $493,000.

Bringing the Burr name aboard was a significant enough accomplishment for the Hills Bank that John Hughes assigned himself to handle the account. Almost immediately, though, the banker felt a twinge. No sooner had he loaned Dale Burr $360,000 than Dale came back and asked for an additional $40,000. Dale Burr told Hughes he wanted the money for his son, John Burr, who had had a bad year. John Hughes agreed to loan the money for six months at 14 percent interest. This was the same rate as the larger loan, but Hughes characteristically insisted that the loan be heavily secured, in this case with both Dale's farm equipment and his crops in the field, when either alone might have been sufficient to carry the obligation.

Dale Burr presented himself at the Hills Bank during the summer of 1984 and made an advance payment of $14,400 on his $360,000 loan. Although this money was not due until March 1985, Dale said he had just sold some corn and wanted to apply the proceeds. A few months later, though, Dale was unable to repay the $40,000 loan for John, and so the bank extended it for another six months. That fall Hughes noted that the Burrs' land had declined in value, like all in the area. A growing tone of displeasure from Hughes was evident the next year when Dale again asked for an extension of the $40,000 for his son. In their conversation on February 8, 1985, Hughes quickly ascertained that Dale had himself loaned his son an additional $20,000, and that Dale did not have the money to pay the interest due on the $360,000 loan due the next month. "Dale needs to borrow $30,000 to pay interest on Real Estate loan financed in March," he wrote in the ledger, concluding that the bank would "need cash flow before any decisions are made by us on above requests."

When the cash-flow statements came in, they did not paint the kind of financial picture that John Hughes liked to be a part of. He took one look, in fact, and delegated the Burr account to a junior assistant, Roger Reilly. Then he gave Reilly his marching instructions. In an early March memorandum, Hughes wrote: "With a severe negative cash flow for both 1984 and 1985, there is obviously no way we can extend any more funds. Be sure that we do not. Next be sure that we have everything presently owing us adequately secured." Hughes suggested that Dale "sell enough land so that the interest payment is eliminated," and concluded, "Obviously, we need to be sure we are adequately secured because the situation can only get worse." In meetings with Dale later that month, Reilly took a hard line. The increasingly alarmed Dale and Emily were essentially at the Hills Bank's mercy, though, since they did not have the money needed to pay the interest on the $360,000 loan they had taken out the year before. The bank was in a position to dictate its own terms, and it did so.

In a March 6 meeting at the bank with Dale and Emily, Hughes led the conversation, much as he had with the hog farmer who wanted to go to Mexico, to the subject of what collateral Dale might be able to offer that would induce the bank to loan him more money. In the parlance of the poker game, he was asking Dale Burr to strip. At length, Dale threw enough on the table to satisfy the banker. As Hughes noted in the bank ledger: "He offered to give us the mortgage on the 160-acre home place and we told him we would loan him that, provided the mortgage on the home place was all-encompassing and secures the entire credit line. Dale said that was fine with him. He will get the abstract out of the safety deposit box and give it to us either later this week or the very first of next week."

The deal that John Hughes cut with Dale and Emily on that March day rivaled the one he had arranged with the railroad annexation in terms of the advantages it imparted to the bank, if not its scope. For $34,000, which was not even an out-of-pocket expense since it represented the interest the Burrs owed, the bank obtained a mortgage to Dale Burr's 160-acre home place, then valued at around $2,000 an acre, or $320,000, not counting the house or any of the outbuildings. In his ledger notes on the transaction, John Hughes wrote, "The reason we are doing this is that we are not extending any additional money, but we are getting 160 acres of additional collateral for the entire credit line. Presently Dale owes us $345,000 on the 240 acres that we have a mortgage on, and while that value is still there our concern is what the situation may be a year from now and what the collateral may be worth then."

No longer able to finance his own operating expenses, Dale was forced to go back to the Hills Bank five days later, March 11, and ask for $5,000 for seed. The request seems to have infuriated John Hughes, for he not only turned Dale down, but let Dale's creditors know that his credit had run out at the Hills Bank. On March 13, John Hughes wrote to Cedar-Johnson Farm Supply that "we are operating under the assumption that Dale will not need to borrow operating funds from our bank this coming year." Roger Reilly meanwhile dressed Dale down for overdrafts in his checking account, telling him "we are not happy" with this. Dale deposited $3,000 into the account to cover the overdrafts, and when he received a $9,600 deficiency payment from the federal government later that spring, he paid $8,000 toward his big note with the Hills Bank. With this and other income, he paid off as many creditors as the money would allow.

But then, in May, Dale was again compelled to approach the Hills Bank about a $5,000 loan for seed corn. On May 16 he came into the Hills Bank and told Roger Reilly that a $5,000 loan was vital to him, as his supplier wanted a check from him when it dropped off the seed. Faced with the prospect of the Burrs' planting no crop that year, the Hills Bank ultimately relented and loaned Dale the $5,000, but Reilly said "we made it very clear to Dale we thought that John [Burr] was going to 'break' him and that we did not think he understood the gravity of the situation."

To try to hammer home the point, John Hughes wrote to Dale and Emily Burr on May 21, 1985, less than three months after they had supposedly taken care of their financial problems by rolling over their big loan with the Hills Bank:

> Lastly, we think it is imperative that we again tell you the severity of your financial situation. It is true that you have substantial assets but you simply cannot go on as you have been and continue to lose money each year because if you do that, it is obvious it is only a matter of time before your assets are exhausted. The cash flow that you projected for this year shows a deficiency of $52,000.00. It seems apparent to us that you simply have to sit down and say we cannot go on like this and must make immediate changes in your farming operation to correct that cash flow. Quite frankly, it appears to us that you are simply going on as before and hoping for better yields and better prices. That simply will not work and you must analyze your farming operation and decide where changes can be made and then implement those changes at once.

We do not want to be in a position of having to foreclose on your farm within the next year but quite frankly, if you do not make changes now, we do not see how that can be avoided. We think you should know that and react accordingly. We realize that all of the problems may not be yours alone and that you have advanced considerable money to John. We have no idea what John's financial situation is but it does appear that he's causing you severe financial problems that could result in you losing your farm if changes are not made and made at once.

We have tried in this letter to once again bring to you the severity of your situation so that you can do something about it. We think it is absolutely imperative that you make immediate changes so that you can continue to farm in the future. However, it is abundantly clear to us that unless those changes are made, there is not much of a future ahead for you. We just don't want you to be surprised by anything that might happen in the future.

Sincerely,
John R. Hughes, President

If Hughes had wanted to get a reaction from the Burrs, he was successful, especially with Emily. Although outwardly as calm as ever, Dale went back into the Hills Bank ten days later and paid $1,000 on the $40,000 loan he had originally taken out for his son one year before. The lack of cooperation among local banks continued to hamper his ability to pay more, however. John Hughes personally called Tom Huston at the Columbus Junction Bank to see if he would release some money from a batch of hogs that John Burr had hocked to the Columbus Junction Bank. Said Huston: "I told him we would not."

Unable to borrow from local banks, Dale began to rely more and more on alternative sources of money. He borrowed against the stock he held with his mother and daughters in the Morris Plan, as well as the bank accounts he controlled for his mother. He also received the dividends on accounts of Julia Burr's, and borrowed from his brother-in-law, Keith Forbes. The past-due notices began to pile up unopened on Dale's desk, and he appears to have begun to gamble. One of Dale's neighbors recalls him saying that he dropped six thousand dollars the day he had some work done on his truck, "three thousand on the truck, and three thousand on the [Chicago] Board of Trade." By July 1985, he had virtually drained the $85,000 in Hilda Burr's bank accounts in Hills, Lone Tree, and Columbus Junction.

A few weeks later, Cedar-Johnson Farm Supply, the Burrs' main supplier of chemicals and fuel, filed liens against Dale and his son totaling more than $50,000. Cedar-Johnson had earlier shown a willingness to wait for their money from Dale (who owned $8,470 of Cedar-Johnson stock), but partly because they had received no payment in over a year, and partly because John Hughes had told them Dale Burr would be getting no operating money from the Hills Bank, the farm supply company decided it had to protect itself. When the Hills Bank learned of the lien a short time later, it was doubly displeased. In the first place, the lien claimed property on which the Hills Bank held an unrestricted first mortgage. Secondly, the lien was another sign of Dale's failure as a farmer in the bank's eyes.

Still, Dale was trying to make the farm work, and trying to change his own methods to make it happen, if that was what it took. In September 1985, he went over to the farm of Archie Buline, a close neighbor to the west, to talk to him about helping combine the Burrs' crop that year. Buline and Dale had been neighbors and friends all their lives, yet Buline remarked that it was the first time Dale had ever asked for help with fieldwork. Turned down for a further loan by the Hills Bank, Dale hit on the scheme of letting the land go temporarily into arrears as a means of indirectly obtaining more credit. "He is willing to pay one percent a month to the [County] Treasurer in lieu of borrowing more money from us," noted a bank official, who added that Dale said he expected to pay his taxes in October or November when he harvested his crop.

On October 2, 1985, Dale came into the Hills Bank with a list of prospective buyers of his farm products requested by the bank. He told John Hughes at the time that he hoped to be able to pay off Cedar-Johnson Farm Supply with grain he sealed with the government that fall. Hughes responded by asking Dale if he had harvested any grain yet. Dale admitted he had not, at which point Hughes refused to discuss the matter further. "I told him I thought it was premature to talk about sealing this year's crop and who he was going to pay," Hughes noted, "and instead suggested that he first get the crop out and then we would know . . . how best to distribute the proceeds. He was reluctant on this because apparently the Farm Service is pressing him pretty hard. . . ." Less than two weeks later, Hughes's fears about Dale Burr's ability to harvest the crop were fueled by a telephone conversation with Keith Forbes.

Forbes told John Hughes that Dale had just been over at his place trying to borrow money or sell feeder pigs for cash. John Hughes understood immediately that Dale's selling pigs for cash almost certainly meant he was trying to secretly unload property that had already been pledged to a bank, and so, in effect, did not belong to the Burrs anymore. If the pigs were John Burr's, they really belonged to the Farmers and Merchants or Columbus Junction bank, and if they were Dale's, they belonged to the Hills Bank, since Dale had signed over all of his produce and crops in the field as part of the collateral for the $40,000 loan he had taken out for his son.

Forbes went on to speculate that Dale's debt to Cedar-Johnson Farm Service might be much larger than Hughes had thought. Additionally, as Hughes recounted the conversation in a confidential memo to the Burrs' account file: "He said that Dale was not going to have any crop this year and hadn't had any for ten years. Keith said he [Dale] did not get his beans in this year until the end of July and then didn't put any fertilizer on and there is simply no bean crop there."

Soon, it became apparent that John Hughes had made a decision on the Burr matter. On November 15, Dale came into the bank to pay the interest on the $5,000 seed loan and ask for an extension on repayment of the principal.

Dale told Roger Reilly that he had harvested 120 acres so far, producing about 18,000 bushels of corn. He had already sealed most of this corn with the federal Agricultural Stabilization and Conservation Service (ASCS), for which he received a $23,000 check.

Government programs like this had been the main source of income for many Midwestern grain farmers since the early 1980s when the bottom fell out of the price of corn. Typically, farmers turned their corn over to the government in the fall. In exchange for their grain, which was sealed in storage until spring, farmers received loans. Later, they could either sell the crop on the open market and pay back the loan, or turn the crop over to the government as payment for the loan.

Dale told Reilly that he hoped to have the harvest finished by Thanksgiving, but for the moment Reilly was more interested in the $23,000 check Dale said he had received from the federal government. Earlier that year the Hills Bank had made what farmers call a "UCC filing" on Dale. The term refers to an Iowa law (Uniform Commercial Code, section 554.9307) that gives creditors the power to require all of a debtor's income to be issued as two-party checks, payable to both the debtor and the creditor.

Farmers, who are the only major group in Iowa subject to such credit legislation, intensely dislike the two-party check statute, for the law has the effect of giving the creditor control over all the debtor's income. "For a factory worker," observed one farmer, "a UCC filing would be the equivalent of having to get two-party checks from their employer if they had a mortgage on their home. Then they'd have to get the bank to co-sign the check before they could cash their paycheck." Somehow, though, Dale had gotten a check without the Hills Bank's name on it.

Reilly asked Dale what he had done with the money. Dale said he had paid Cedar-Johnson Farm Service and some other creditors, as well as his real-estate taxes. Some of the money apparently also went to John Burr, although it is not clear whether Dale told the Hills Bank about this. Finally, the few thousand dollars that remained were deposited in the Burrs' account at the Hills Bank. Dale's payment of his real-estate taxes meant that he had gotten his land out of hock from the county assessor without borrowing money from the Hills Bank, as he had hoped.

Reilly, however, quickly dampened that hope. He indicated that the check from the ASCS was not Dale's money, and immediately put a hold on Dale's account so that no checks could be paid without the bank's approval. Dale pleaded for payment of at least the real-estate tax check he had just written, but Reilly refused to say whether the bank would release the money or not. Likewise, he would not say what the bank's decision on the question of the loan extension would be, but he hinted Dale should not get his hopes up. "I told him since the $5,000 he had borrowed for seed was due on Friday," Reilly wrote in a memo to John Hughes, "they might want it paid but I would check with you and let him know."

Then Reilly asked Hughes how to proceed. "Do we want to go along with him as long as we can?" he continued in his memo. "Or should we have him pay the notes as they come due and not extend anything?" When Hughes heard the latest developments on the Burr account, he was furious. Even though the bank held more than enough collateral for the $40,000 loan for John Burr without that one portion of Dale's crop, he treated the incident as an abomination. He scrawled in the margin beside Reilly's description of the $23,000 ASCS check affair, "How the hell did this happen?"

Thus driven by their leader, Reilly and bank vice-president Tim Smith had a tough meeting with Dale and Emily on Friday of that week, November 19. First off, Dale was told he would get no extension. The $5,000 was due immediately, even though he had not yet harvested all of the crop produced by the seed. Reviewing Dale and Emily's overall situation, the bank officers noted a $360,000 decrease in net worth over the last five years, and a corresponding increase in debt during that same period. The bankers did not mention that Dale had also paid large sums to the banks, including $112,000 to the Hills Bank during 1984 and 1985 alone. They were more interested in the fact that he projected a $9,000 negative cash flow for the year, and was still unable to repay the $40,000 loan for John.

Informing the Burrs that they did not have "enough current assets to pay his current liabilities," Smith and Reilly strongly suggested they "give serious thought to liquidating the horses and consider selling the farm equipment and renting the land for 1986." In this discussion Smith took the lead. A large man with a softness in the middle that made his dark suit coat draw tight wrinkle chevrons when buttoned, he emphasized the dire consequences that could befall the Burrs if they did not tighten their belts. While trying to be firm enough to make the Burrs confront their situation realistically, Smith also wanted to provide Dale and Emily with the sort of positive solution to their dilemma for which the Hills Bank was noted.

"We believe Dale should liquidate his current assets and his equipment and pay his current liabilities," Reilly wrote of the meeting, "and then rent the land out and make his real-estate payments from rental income." Smith and Reilly tried to present this course of action as prudent in that it would provide against further debt erosion of the family's holdings, and allow Dale and Emily to retire on the home place. For Dale, however, what they were proposing meant something else. You could coat it with fancy words, but when you got down to it, they were telling him to get out, telling him he could not farm anymore.

Meanwhile, Tom Huston, president of the Columbus Junction State Bank, called a big chunk of the Burrs' loan for the Parizek place. According to the bank, the general decline in Iowa real-estate values meant John Burr's net worth was $53,000, rather than the $373,000 he figured in a recent report to the bank. Huston said the bank would only renew $100,000 of the Burrs' $139,000 loan with the bank when it came due. This meant that Dale and John had to come up with another $39,000. In conclusion, Huston apologized for giving the Burrs less than a month's notice. Like the small loans with the Hills Bank, the money was due at the end of November.

Dale worked on Thanksgiving, but many acres remained unharvested when he knocked off for family dinner, which was traditionally held at Emily's sister's in nearby Tipton. That night the weather turned ugly. Freezing rain and sleet were followed by heavy snow. The snow made harvest next to impossible, and the cold rendered the stalks as brittle as old glass. Even if you could get out in the fields, the wastage was much higher. As the blizzard bore down, sweeping in out of the north and gathering in long sinuous drifts behind the outbuildings, Dale sat in the house fretting.

The day after Thanksgiving, with the blizzard howling outside, the ASCS wrote Dale to inform him that it would foreclose on the two loans he had just received for his sealed corn unless he could work something out with the Hills Bank. Now Dale faced being barred from further participation in the ASCS program. At a time when the government subsidy programs were the principal source of income available to American grain farmers, this was the equivalent of the banishment among the ice floes by the Eskimos. If Dale could not seal corn and could not sell it, then all of his other obligations would be impossible to meet. He would lose everything he had borrowed on, which was everything he owned.

Dale had thought for some time that the Hills Bank was not making it any easier to keep his head above water financially. Now he began to think that the banks in Hills, Lone Tree, and Columbus Junction were actively conspiring to bring about his downfall. The obvious reason, it must have occurred to him in a dark moment, was that he was worth more to the banks "dead than alive." That is, he was so overpledged with collateral that he was worth much more to the bank as a foreclosure than he was as a good customer. Why else, he may have wondered, would the Hills Bank block every effort he made to dig himself out, and seem so steadfastly hostile from almost the very moment it had his signature putting a mortgage on the home place?

In a late-November outburst that struck Keith Forbes as uncharacteristically venomous, Dale referred to Tim Smith at the Hills Bank as "that beady-eyed S.O.B." Dale, of course, was not the only farmer feeling hostility toward his banker during the winter of 1985. The number of federal farm foreclosures had doubled over the last year, involving a total of some two thousand farms and a half-million acres nationwide. In the Midwest particularly, farmers were feeling the pressure from public and private lenders. Said Dean Goldsmith of Corning, Iowa, who lost both his farm and his marriage, "You can't believe what these lenders do to people. They get you feeling so low you can go out the door without opening it." Gary Dolan, a Chillicothe, Missouri, farmer who went bankrupt and then worked his way back, remembered with anger the bankers' questioning his management skills. "He's sitting behind his desk playing with a Rubik's Cube, and his secretary is outside knitting booties for her grandchild, and he's telling me, 'You've got to be more efficient.' "

The banks, for their part, argued that they did not control the international grain market, or the weather. "The whole picture changed in four years," said Larry Evers, vice-president and farm manager for the First National Bank of Dwight, Illinois. "Four years ago the people who were successful were buying land, creating debt. These are the people who are being hurt very badly today. Farmland has gone from a top price of $4,000 an acre around here to about $1,500. . . . The buyers owe more than the land is worth." As a result, federal bank examiners forced banks to call a portion of their farm loans. In fact, the Columbus Junction's decision to call $39,000 of Dale and John Burr's $139,000 loan was prompted in this manner.

Nor were the losses suffered by banks insignificant. Many bankers were pushed to the brink with the farmers they backed, and suffered similar trauma and humiliation. In most cases, small-town agricultural bankers were not dealing with impersonal loan accounts, but with people they had known all their lives. The closeness of the emotional bond between bankers and farmers is underscored by the case of Gordon Geiken of Vinton, Iowa, a banker who committed suicide rather than foreclose on friends in the fall of 1985.

Dale Burr was not in a position to be too concerned about this, though. What he saw was a pack of fast talkers stealing a century of his family's sweat. He had no political or ideological means of rationalizing his outrage, but he knew he was being destroyed and the basic code of his life was being violated. He knew they were closing in on him too, for he could see their soft faces and smell their sweet, mint-scented breath.

Dale Burr approached the Hills Bank for the second time a little before eleven-thirty that morning. Bank officer Dale Kretchmar noticed Dale as he walked past outside his window, and said to Reilly, "Dale Burr is coming in."

"Again?" Reilly replied. "He was just here."

Upon reentering the back door of the Hills Bank, Dale walked down the short hall to the point where it opens on the main lobby and, to the right, John Hughes's office.

Dale was limping, as if he had slipped on the ice outside, one person thought. He paused outside Hughes's door and peered through the little window.

Several bank employees noticed Dale standing outside John Hughes's office, but they thought he must be waiting to talk to Hughes. One of the tellers saw Dale bend over and appear to unzip his coveralls. "Look, he's opening the door to John's office," said Denise Maier, the teller whom Dale had dealt with a quarter-hour before.

Inside, John Hughes was discussing bank business with his comptroller, James Pratt. Pratt handed Hughes a slip of paper with some information he wanted, and sat back in his chair by the window. Just then the door opened a few inches and stopped. Assuming it was another bank officer who had been detained in the hall by someone else, Hughes and Pratt turned back to their conversation.

Dale Burr was one of the last things on John Hughes's mind at that moment, for there were no immediate dead-lines concerning him at the bank that day. John Hughes's attention was focused on matters of the moment: Pratt's data, the ever-ringing phone, the agenda of the upcoming meeting of the Hillsbancorp board of directors, and a great deal more. Swiveling back and forth in his big chair, he was a picture of the persuasive power of money.

Just then, Dale pulled the 12-gauge out of his coverall leg and raised it. Almost simultaneously, Pratt noticed the barrel of a shotgun draw a bead through the crack in the door, and Sue Barnhill, John Hughes's secretary, looked up to see Dale aiming the gun into Hughes's office. She cried, "DALE, don't do that!" just as he fired one round into the back of John Hughes's head from nearly point-blank range. The shot blew off most of the left side of the banker's head, splattering blood, bone, flesh, and brain all across his office and stippling his window red with what looked like holiday decorations. Pratt took one look at the slumped figure of John Hughes, with a little remnant of his left ear hanging below the awful void that had been his head and face, and knew that first aid was unnecessary.

Elsewhere in the bank, the explosion went unrecognized for several long moments. One bank employee thought it was a light bulb breaking, and several more thought it was the sound of a filing cabinet falling over. Shortly, however, the bank employees realized it was a shot, and that the person who fired it was still in the bank. On the other side of the atrium, receptionist Barbara Mahanna pushed a button to summon police. Suddenly people all over the bank were panicking, tripping over each other and ducking for cover. B. D. Duwa, a farmer from nearby Kalona, Iowa, was three doors down from John Hughes's office "talking about this and that." Duwa said he thought someone was robbing the bank by the way bank employees "started running around pressing buttons." There was no armed guard on duty at the Hills Bank that morning.

Still standing by the door to John Hughes's office with the shotgun in his hand, Dale Burr turned to leave. Then, as if he had another thought, he walked a few steps to the office where Roger Reilly had refused to cash the five-hundred-dollar check a few minutes before. Reilly was talking to Dale Kretchmar when Dale Burr appeared at the door and pointed the gun at him, declaring, "I'm going to get you too." Reilly paled and his eyes widened. Then Dale experienced something about which many oppressed farmers have fantasized. He held a gun on a banker who had helped torment him and listened while the man begged for his life. "Dale, please, you can't do this." Then, in the batting of an eye, Kretchmar knocked the barrel of Dale's gun up with his arm, and Reilly dove under his desk. Dale might have killed Kretchmar right then, but he did not.

Instead, he backed out of Reilly's office. Pausing for a moment on the other side of the glass, he stared directly into Kretchmar's eyes and then turned around. Some bank employees had the terrible feeling at that moment that Dale was going to shoot others in the bank lobby, but he calmly returned the way he had come, toward Hughes's office and the back door. This spread further panic, however, for many had tried to flee out the back door, clogging the hall in their effort to get away. Now the last of this crowd found itself pinned between the door and the advancing gunman. Witnesses say that Dale almost stumbled and fell over the people desperately scattering in front of him.

Outside, Dale threw his gun on the seat of the truck, climbed in, and started the engine. By now there was a small crowd standing in the parking lot. As he pulled away, Dale gazed back at them with the dry-eyed look of a man who lives in the land of clear and irrevocable justice. Inside the Hills Bank, distraught bank employees were already on the phone giving law-enforcement officers an account of what had just happened, but they did not know the half of it.

PART THREE

Woe to those who add house to house
and join field to field
until everywhere belongs to them
and they are the sole inhabitants of the land.
Isaiah 5:8

7

Dale Burr drove out of Hills on the main street, heading back the way he had come a half hour before. The sky was an even gray and the broad landscape was almost entirely drained of color. Dirty snow, dead corn stubble, and an occasional white farmhouse were all he saw. It seemed to be turning colder, and a little snow was ticking on the windshield.

At the junction of Highway W-66, which goes north to Iowa City, and F-62, which goes southeast to Lone Tree, Dale headed straight toward Lone Tree. A mile farther, he turned onto a secondary section line road and followed the tracks running on the snow for a mile to a remote junction. Here he turned again, and stopped his green four-wheel-drive pickup in the middle of the road.

Reaching across the seat, he picked up his shotgun and examined it, working the pump several times. In the bank, he thought the gun might have jammed on him. Now he had to find out whether it was working before he proceeded. So once again he filled the magazine of his old model 31, shoving the shiny brass and green plastic shells home with his work-hardened thumb. He did not bother to turn the engine off as he stepped out and fired a couple of shots in the air.

Apparently satisfied, he got back in the truck and drove off at high speed into the maze of section line roads that crisscross rural Johnson County. Most of these local right-of-ways are unpaved, and many are dead ends due to wash-outs. Although seldom traveled in winter—especially by law-enforcement officers from Iowa City—a man with good local knowledge and four-wheel-drive could travel unnoticed on them for hundreds of miles in any direction.

At that very moment, in fact, a Johnson County Sheriff's Department patrol car was speeding toward Hills on the main road near where Dale was speeding in the other direction on the back roads. Dale could have gotten away then, could have gone to Lone Tree or Columbus Junction, but he had a closer objective in mind. As he neared his destination, he could see a farm three-quarters of a mile to the north. There were a couple dozen structures, ranging from a good-sized barn down to little sheds, some of which were barely wide enough to be an outhouse. Beyond, nestled in a pine windbreak at the top of a slight rise, stood a modest white bungalow.

This was the late Paul Goody's farm, now the home of his son Richard. Like Burr, Goody is an old Johnson County name with roots going back to the previous century, when a Mrs. Pauline Goody was among the Johnson County Civil War soldiers' wives receiving aid from the public relief fund. Upright and hard-working, they too had found their Land of Canaan on the Iowa plains. Just as Dale, Lloyd Jr., and John Burr controlled land northeast of Lone

Tree, so the Goodys—Richard, Jim, and Marvin—controlled about a mile of frontage on F-62 over toward Hills.

The Goodys were primarily corn, soybean, and hog farmers, like the Burrs, but there were several important differences between the families. One was religion. While the Burrs were Lutherans, the Goodys were Catholics. The Goodys were in the majority in this respect, for St. Joseph's Catholic Church, where the Goodys were regular worshipers, is easily the largest church in Hills. The Burrs, by contrast, had to drive to Iowa City to attend a Missouri Synod Lutheran church, and there the congregation was made up more of people from town businesses and the University of Iowa than country people and farmers.

Both the Goody and Burr farms might appear prosperous to a casual visitor, but there were crucial distinctions that Johnson County residents could see at a glance. In the first place, the Goody house was too small and too new to stand beside some of the really grand old farmhouses that dot the landscape between Hills and Lone Tree. It was not the kind of structure that anyone was likely to have photographed and included in a regional history, as Nelson Burr had done with the house where Dale grew up. Secondly, although the Goodys owned hundreds of acres of choice Iowa farmland, they did not own enough to operate independently. As a result, Paul Goody and his son Richard had to rent land: They were tenant farmers.

One piece they rented was the eighty-acre Parizek place over in Section 26 between the Dale Burr and Harold Schuessler farms. Goody and Leslie Parizek, who had been forced to retire from farming due to health problems, had an oral crop-share agreement. Each man paid half the cost of seed and fertilizer, and Parizek paid for lime. When the crop was harvested, Goody and Parizek each took half. The

Parizek place was farther from the Goodys' home place than he might have hoped, but Paul Goody, who began farming there around 1960, was glad to have the use of such rich land, and glad to have it on terms that minimized the up-front capital he was required to provide.

Still, the fact remained that Paul Goody was beholden to another man for some of the earth he farmed. Working on an oral agreement, he could be evicted or have the terms of the lease altered on him. He could not plan freely, nor could he reap the full reward of his labors. While Parizek paid part of the capital costs, Goody did all the work for half the money. Like tenant farmers everywhere, Goody had a smaller profit margin than farmers who owned all their own land. He had to be better than his neighbors— shrewder, stronger, able to work longer hours—just to hold his own. Even then, the Goodys were one step removed from being pushed off the land.

In America, tenancy has long provided an avenue to farm ownership, but the path has also been well-trodden in the other direction. During the last century, especially, farm tenancy in America has steadily grown, while the percentage of farmers who own their own farms has steadily declined. In 1880, 25 percent of all American farmers were tenants; by 1890, tenant farmers had grown to 28 percent; by 1900, 35 percent were tenants; by 1910, 37 percent. The following decade was one of the most prosperous in U.S. history, the period of America's first vital rise as an imperial power, when expanding markets and the advantages of larger exploitation quickened the national economy. These were especially good years for many American farmers, but for tenant farmers they were perilous. Always among the first victims in hard times, tenant farmers have actually been more vulnerable in some ways during good times.

The dilemma of tenants during the World War I boom is dramatically portrayed in Sophus K. Winther's novel of farming on the Nebraska plains, *This Passion Never Dies*. In 1917, near the top of the incredible price run-up that saw farmland reach highs it would not attain again for fifty years, the hero, a Scandinavian immigrant tenant farmer named Peter Grimsen, gambled by taking out a large mortgage to buy the farm he had been renting. Land prices had been rising steadily since the Crash of 1893, and Grimsen was afraid that if he did not buy the place someone else would. Like thousands of other American farmers, Grimsen was also swayed by the patriotic appeals from the federal government aimed at increasing farm output during a time of war.

A variety of price inducements were offered, but probably the most significant step the federal government took to encourage farm expansion during World War I was the creation of the Land Bank system, which greatly liberalized farm credit and helped reform what Thorstein Veblen called "notoriously usurious" American farm loan practices. In 1917, the first year the nation was involved in the war, record acreage was planted to food in the U.S. Three years later, in 1920, the full impact of the American agricultural buildup was felt when the largest corn crop then on record was harvested. Under the weight of the American bounty (and the increased food production around the world, especially in Canada, Australia, and Argentina), the price for agricultural products plummeted during the summer of 1920. Between November 1 and December 10 of that year, the price of beef on the hoof fell by nearly half. Many prime steers showed a loss of fifty to a hundred dollars a head that year.

The 1920 crop had been produced at a higher cost than any in the nation's history, and after the back-breaking labor of hauling in a record harvest, it turned out in many cases that the proceeds would not even cover out-of-pocket expenses, let alone provide the farmer with an income. Although overproduction was the acknowledged cause of the Midwestern grain farmers' problems, these same farmers saw no alternative but to plant even more. Since they were running on a declining margin, the only way to increase their total return was to increase their volume. If they had not been so deeply in debt for land and machinery, they might have cut back and ridden it out, but most farmers lacked that option. Without cash income they would lose their farms to foreclosure, yet to obtain cash they were forced to follow a course of action that was collectively ruinous.

The collapse of the price of corn led to a rash of farm foreclosures that swept thousands of heavily indebted farmers like Peter Grimsen off the land. Although delayed slightly by World War I, the American agricultural crash of 1920 clearly illustrated the continuing power of the twenty-year cycle that had ruled the nineteenth-century farm economy. Falling twenty-seven years after the Crash of 1893, and a hundred and one years after the Crash of 1819, the Crash of 1920 was caused by the same combination of overproduction and heavy debt that helped trigger its five predecessors.

Significantly, the 1920 census showed that farmers were in the minority for the first time in the United States' history. There were still approximately 32 million people living on 6.5 million farms, but both totals were declining daily. Between 1920 and 1930, six hundred thousand people left the farm annually, for a total migration away from rural America of six million people over ten years, or nearly 20 percent. The frontier was by then only a memory of old men. The process of enclosure now drove the majority of the best and the brightest not west, but into the cities. Seeking opportunity and wider cultural horizons, many of these people played a prominent role in creating the dynamic modern urban American culture that first emerged during the 1920s and 1930s.

Back on the farm, the culture they left behind was dying, although like a cow in the early stages of milk fever, the severity of the situation was not entirely evident. Many farm communities seemed vigorous, and most of the work was still done by hand and horse power. The continued popularity of horses was due partly to the fact that tractors were then still relatively limited in capacity (they could not yet efficiently plant or cultivate), and partly to the farmer's conviction that horses were fundamentally cheaper. Since the feed it took to operate horses could be grown by the farmer, unlike gasoline and oil, many farmers figured the value of horses as much in the flexibility they allowed as the straight dollar return.

As the dollar return became more important, though, farmers that increasingly sold on the idea that they could pay for the additional cost of machinery through increased production and decreased labor costs. It was also extremely attractive to think of eliminating some of the back-breaking physical labor that had been a part of farming since before the ancient Egyptians built the pyramids. The marvelous new machinerey did in fact increase production and decrease labor costs, but what the farmers had not foreseen was that their collective shifting of twenty-five million acres of work-animal pasture to cash crops would drive some agricultural prices still lower.

As the pressure mounted, many on the edge cut back ruthlessly on their efforts at husbandry. Tenants, especially, who had no long-term interest in the land, were notorious for wasting the soil. "The serious defect of our system of tenantry is the lack of suitable provisions for maintaining the fertility of the soil," observed the U.S. Department of Agriculture Yearbook in 1916. By the mid-1920s, government studies showed that prime, rolling farmland like that along the Mississippi in southeastern Iowa was annually losing in excess of five tons of top soil per acre. Nationally, America was losing 126 billion pounds of active soil nutrients annually, worth an estimated $2 billion at the cheapest fertilizer costs of 1928.

Soil erosion also had its direct counterpart in the erosion of society. Especially in the poorer and more marginal areas, such as on the arid edge of the Western plains, the social lattice that had made farm communities strong was beginning to break down and crumble away. In some areas of the Great Plains that were originally settled by homesteaders, the majority of farmers were tenants by the late 1920s, and the majority of those had been on their current places only a few years. Young people like Peter Grimsen's son Hans were especially disinclined to put down roots in rural communities.

While most of the American economy rebounded from the crash of 1920 during the "Roaring Twenties," the farm sector did not generally share in this bounty, even though production remained high. By the mid-1920s, American farmers were once again rising in outrage. The new ferment started in the West and spread south and east. The Corn Belt remained relatively unmoved until the price of hogs fell to pre–World War I levels in 1923. Then Iowa reacted dramatically, electing the most radical senator in its history, Smith W. (for Wildman) Brookhart, who advocated public ownership of railroads and refused to support his party's champion, Calvin Coolidge, for president. Another Iowa congressman, Representative Gilbert Haugen, was co-sponsored the decade's most controversial farm bill.

The McNary-Haugen Act was a product of the growing sophistication of agrarian thinking, and represented a sort of cross-pollination between progressive and conservative farm thought. The direct inspiration came from *A Plan for Equality in Agriculture,* an influential 1922 treatise on the farm problem by Moline Plow Company officials George Peek and Hugh Johnson. Decrying the fact that America had become "a nation of wage earners and tenants tending toward peasantry," Peek and Johnson blamed hidden subsidies to industry (in the form of tariffs) for the farmers' woes. The McNary-Haugen Act was designed to remedy this historic imbalance, and put America's agricultural produce on an equal tariff footing with industry.

Support for the McNary-Haugen Act came from a broad political spectrum, but was solidly rooted in the center. The so-called farm bloc, a bipartisan congressional farm caucus founded by Iowa Senator W. S. Kenyon, threw its considerable establishment weight behind the act, as did the newly founded Farm Bureau Federation, whose members tended to be conservative on nonfarm issues such as municipal ownership of utilities, which they opposed. Many of the farmers who clamored for passage of the McNary-Haugen Act were the sort of staunch Republicans who had fought for the Union and sent William Jennings Bryan down to defeat. Now, in their hour of crisis, they found certain of their Republican brethren implacably hostile.

Twice, in 1927 and 1928, Congress passed the McNary-Haugen Act, and twice President Calvin Coolidge vetoed the measure. In ignoring the plaint of loyal Republican farmers, Coolidge brought American history to a point the

English had arrived at eighty years before when Conservative Prime Minister Robert Peel repealed the Corn Laws, which were England's ancient tariff protection for its native farmers. In both cases, the farmers who had supported the conservative establishment were betrayed on crucial tariff issues as soon as they no longer represented a popular majority, and the fundamental power of the nation shifted to the urban populace. Neither the Conservatives nor the Republicans escaped unscathed politically, however.

Prime Minister Peel was forced to resign within a month, and although the process took a little longer in the United States, the effect was much the same. President Coolidge and his Republican successor, Herbert Hoover, drove farmers en masse into the Democratic fold. By the early 1930s, A. N. Young, president of the Wisconsin Farmers Union, could declare, "The farmer is naturally a conservative individual, but you can't find a conservative farmer today." The defection of long-standing Republicans in rural America was crucial to the success of Democrat Franklin D. Roosevelt's bid for the presidency in 1932.

In repayment, Roosevelt pushed several agricultural acts through Congress during the first one hundred days of the New Deal. The most significant was undoubtedly the revolutionary Agricultural Adjustment Act. For the first time, the government had the authority to set mandatory production levels to protect prices and prevent overproduction. The Agricultural Adjustment Act of 1933 also significantly liberalized farm credit and—perhaps most interesting of all—adjusted the proportion of gold and silver in U.S. currency, essentially inflating the dollar as Bryan had sought four decades before.

Although declared unconstitutional by the U.S. Supreme Court, the act was passed again in 1938. The second version of the act strove to produce an "ever normal granary" through a system of loans, acreage allotments, and marketing quotas for basic crops such as corn. As Secretary of Agriculture Henry A. Wallace observed, "Fundamentally there are just two ways of reducing production. One is by what is termed free-market prices. The other is through a national program which will enable farmers to make the proper adjustments cooperatively."

Having seen enough of the boom-bust cycle associated with the free-market system, Wallace steered the U.S. Department of Agriculture, and the United States as a whole, toward cooperative (if mandatory) restraint. Wallace, a native Iowan, also directed the American government's first large-scale attack on social and soil erosion, which were then so evident in the Dust Bowl and Appalachia. During Wallace's tenure, farmers were paid not to grow crops for the first time, and food stamps were instituted as a means of putting the nation's staggering agricultural surplus in the hands of the needy.

Although subsequently bowdlerized and turned to entirely different ends than originally envisioned, the basic New Deal system of governmentally administered price and production controls were in effect for nearly a half-century. All Dale's adult life these controls were as much a part of the landscape of Iowa farming as thunderheads in the afternoon.

In fact, governmental control of Midwestern grain farmers did not effectively end until the early 1970s, about the time Dale took over leadership of the Burr family farm enterprise from his father.

Dale slowed his truck to a deliberate crawl as he neared the Goodys' outlying hog-farrowing sheds. Turning left at the mailbox, he headed straight down the Goodys' drive past the house and parked in the yard.

There was no one at the house, but Dale's arrival did not go unnoticed. In small rural communities like Lone Tree, everyone knows everyone else at a distance by the vehicle they drive. Often, the sound of a particular truck or tractor is enough to identify its owner.

Friends frequently dropped by the Goodys', but the Burrs were not among those who normally paid social visits. Rich Goody probably tensed a little when he recognized Dale's pickup. John Burr had evicted Rich from the Parizek place in 1982, prompting an acrimonious lawsuit between the two.

Rich had not had direct contact with any of the Burrs since, but lately he had heard that the Burrs were in some financial difficulty. His curiosity aroused, Rich walked across the barnyard.

Wiry and clean-shaven, Rich was then a thirty-eight-year-old father of two young children. A self-effacing sort of person, he was too private to reveal himself easily, and too hard a worker to have much time for casual socializing. People who knew him well appreciated him as a true friend, though.

One neighbor, Duane Brun, recalled the time his baler broke in the middle of a custom haying job. Brun, who had a reputation of never missing a job, figured he was knocked out. In fact, he had just given up and was headed into the house when Rich drove up. Hearing what was afoot, Rich insisted that the two of them fix the broken baler themselves right then.

"Rich really didn't like to change oil or work with machinery," Brun said. "He did it, but it wasn't his thing, if you know what I mean." Nonetheless Rich and Duane worked that Sunday night until nearly midnight on Brun's big round baler, tearing the implement down and removing a sheared part. Then they welded a repair and reinstalled it. Duane was ready to bale again the next day, and it never would have happened without Rich Goody.

On his own, Rich was a model of efficiency. It was typical that he had already finished harvesting his corn and beans by Thanksgiving and had turned to other chores. The snow that was tormenting Dale was not a problem for Rich, since he was not still struggling to try to get his crop out of the field. Instead, he was ready to take advantage of the weather by hauling out manure, which requires that the fields be frozen in the winter.

In fact, Rich had just returned from spreading manure on the fields behind the house. Driving in, Dale would have known this immediately, for the tractor and manure spreader were parked in the yard by the hog house. It was nearly lunchtime, and Rich had come in to eat with his wife and young son, who were due home from a shopping trip to Hills. At that moment, though, about 11:40 A.M., Rich was alone.

Dale got out of his green and white truck and waited for Rich as he approached. The two men's dress was so similar that they could almost have been soldiers in the same army. Like Dale, Rich Goody was dressed in green coveralls and a red farmer's cap with a feed logo. To this, he added a red down jacket, work gloves, and boots covered with rubber overshoes.

Standing there by the Goodys' machine shed, Dale gave no immediate cause for alarm. Rich did not know Dale's business, but he clearly did not expect any trouble. As he drew close, Rich pulled off his right glove to shake Dale's hand.

8

For twenty years, pictures of John Burr and Rich Goody have been safely locked together under plastic. They are part of the roster of past graduates that Lone Tree High School displays in its front entryway.

John Burr's graduation photograph for the class of 1965 shows a kid with dimples and a butch haircut. His face was strong and handsome, but there was a shyness in his eyes, and a hint of complexity.

John's photo appears near the top of the page, among the class leaders. He was president of the Lone Tree chapter of Future Farmers of America, an honor society member, and past president of his class, as well as an adept athlete and a member of the glee club. With his native ability and his family's long-standing importance in Johnson County, John Burr's future seemed as bright as his ambitions. As a senior, he announced his intention to own a thousand acres.

On the other side of the oversized page, John's photo is almost exactly back to back with that of his sister, Sheila.

Like her older brother, Sheila Burr was a prominent member of the student body the year she graduated, 1966. She was Homecoming Queen, an excellent student, and the most gifted graphic artist the school had seen in many years. Most of the boys in Sheila Burr's class held her in a kind of otherworldly awe, including a slight fellow named Rich Goody, whose photo appeared near the bottom of the same page.

Rich Goody's portrait is not one of the first that the eye falls upon, either because of its position or his appearance. Rich had a thin face with a prominent nose. The part in his neatly combed sandy hair was neatly combed, but the part wandered a little like the furrow left by a plow on a side hill. Although his brow was a trifle heavy and his chin chiseled with a dimple, his most striking feature, and the one that animated all the rest, was the slight but discernible twist of humor in the corners of his mouth.

Rich was a member of the Lone Tree chapter of Future Farmers of America the year when John Burr was president. Although they worked together on several FFA projects, the two were not personally close. In fact, few people outside the Goody family knew Rich well. Unless provoked, he had very little to say, either in class or out. Nor was he much involved in sports or other extracurricular activities apart from FFA. Unlike some of his classmates, he was unable to devote his afternoons to pleasure. His family needed him at home to help with the farm work.

Rich's father, Paul Goody, taught him that if you wanted to succeed in farming you had to keep your eyes peeled. The elder Goody was one of those people who was always finding some way to make a little extra or save on expenses. He did work for others, and sold seeds, as some farmers do, to reduce his own seed costs. Over the years,

Paul developed a reputation for thoroughness and thoughtfulness that brought customers back. He was, for instance, the only seed dealer between Lone Tree and Hills who routinely tested to confirm the germination rates stamped on the sacks by the seed companies. "That's what all those funny little buildings at the Goodys' were for," recalled one old farmer. "He ran tests on everything he sold. That's the kind of man he was."

Paul Goody passed on to his sons an almost reverential attitude toward farm equipment that harkened back to early days on the Great Plains, when pioneers sometimes brought their most prized possession—their plow—in the house with them for safekeeping. He was not crazy to own the latest of everything, but he absolutely insisted on certain basic things, like putting the equipment away clean. A lot of people pay lip service to this old dictum, but the Goodys did it. You never saw any equipment of the Goodys' left out rusting in the rain. Paul Goody taught his sons well, for even after he died, they kept their implements so clean that it embarrassed some of their neighbors.

Like Rich Goody, John Burr learned farming from his family. He studied his grandfather's deft scythe strokes as he trimmed the long grass along a fence line, and observed his father's finesse on a tractor. Dale and Vernon were demanding masters, and John proved a quick study. By the time he was a teenager, he was raising champion shorthorn cattle. Dale always stressed doing a good job, but because of the Burrs' greater resources, that meant something different to them than it did to the Goodys. Having prospered by growing larger for the better part of a century, the Burrs were believers in that primal American adage: Big is better.

To the Burrs, size of operation was a measure of pride. They always had a lot of whatever they were raising, although not always with the desired result. Neighbors still talk about the time that Dale and John were back behind the barn working with the sheep. Noticing smoke rising from the barn, a neighbor driving by stopped at the house and pointed it out to Emily. She called the Lone Tree Volunteer Fire Department, which arrived with sirens blazing about the time Dale and John emerged from behind the barn to see what all the excitement was about. It turned out that there was no fire at all. Dale and John had been docking the tails of lambs, and the iron had ignited some of the wool. There were so many lamb tails in the pile that the smoke could be seen a half-mile away.

After graduating from Lone Tree High School, John Burr attended one of the nation's most prestigious agricultural schools, Iowa State University. Later, like John Hughes, he transferred to the University of Iowa in Iowa City, which was more liberal-arts oriented, and located only a dozen miles from Lone Tree. During much of his time at the University of Iowa, John Burr lived in a trailer court between Iowa City and Lone Tree. Although he frequently ate and did his laundry at home, he was not much involved in the community of Lone Tree, with one memorable exception.

"There had been a rash of gas siphoning for some time," a friend recalled. "Kids were sneaking in and stealing their cruising gas out of farmers' tanks, figuring they would never notice. Well, of course people did notice, but they didn't get caught until one weekend at the Burrs'." The kids knew the schedules of the people whose gas they were siphoning. And so on that Saturday when Dale and Emily were at the high school watching a ball game, they planned to visit the Burr place. What they didn't know was that John was home. Partway through, he heard them. Grabbing his gun, he ran downstairs and yelled at them to freeze. The kids panicked and tried to get away. They roared past John as he fired a shot that blew out a tire. None of the thieves was injured, but they raised a flap over the shot. In the end, a neighbor recalled that the Burrs had to buy them a new tire.

Like most of the men in his family, John Burr was accustomed to using a gun. He had hunted pheasants since he was a boy and later received additional training in the Army Reserves, which he joined during the late 1960s. Among the many reasons for joining the Reserves, one that was not lost on college students then was the draft exemption it offered. A person could trade six years of summer duty Stateside for two years of fighting overseas in an unpopular war. Rich Goody, who had gone to work on the family farm full-time as soon as he graduated from high school, was not so fortunate. Before his twentieth birthday, Rich received an induction notice from the U.S. Army.

The Goodys had no desire for Rich to avoid service, yet it was obvious that this was a particularly bad time for him to be gone. He was both more competent and more needed than ever before as his father got older. If Paul Goody felt any bitterness over Rich being taken from them, it was not directed toward the American leaders who had launched the nation on an undeclared war. It was members of the community who managed to avoid the most hazardous military service that aroused his ire.

After Rich finished training, the Goodys' preliminary fears were confirmed. He was shipped to Vietnam, where he saw battle duty in the aftermath of the Tet Offensive. His artillery unit was in the thick of several desperate engagements, but the one that struck him most was one he missed. Sent out to have some dental work done, Rich was away from the front for a couple days. When he returned, he found most of his unit had been killed. Even though he saw death close up on the farm, he was staggered by this experience. It took days for the reality to sink in, and even then it marked him. One friend recalled of Rich after he returned from Vietnam: "He felt he was living on borrowed time."

Rich Goody saw things in the jungles of Southeast Asia that he never dreamed of a few months before. Mayhem and misery were rampant, and sometimes the living paid a greater price than the dead. He was particularly affected by the children in Vietnam. Everywhere he went he saw the children, begging and maimed, as the real victims of the war. Like many G-Is, he gave candy bars and first-aid kits to young Vietnamese. More than anything else, the war made Rich appreciate the quiet virtues of Iowa life. After Vietnam, he had no desire to do anything but go home and put down roots in the rich country between Lone Tree and Hills.

The Goodys felt their prayers had been answered when Rich was discharged from active duty in the Army in 1969. He was in one piece physically, but it was hard to gauge his deeper emotional condition. "If he was quiet before he went to Vietnam," remembered one friend, "he was twice as quiet afterward." Wanting to put the war behind him, Rich began to immerse himself in the family farm operation. Neighbor and relative Carroll Eden recalled Rich was a demon worker after the war. "He was a hard-working boy," said Eden. "He never took a vacation."

The thing that started to bring Rich out of himself was a disastrous double date. The girl whom Rich was supposed to go out with got sick at the last minute, and so he ended up on a blind date with someone else who definitely was not his style. The evening was not a total loss, though. Rich was struck by his friend's date, a slight, brown-haired woman named Marilyn. She had grown up on a farm in northwest Iowa, and was working as a nurse in Iowa City. He called her a couple of days later, and before long they had fallen deeply in love.

Rich and Marilyn were wed on January 6, 1973, in Iowa City. Marilyn had wanted to get married in the Catholic church in Hills, but it did not work out. The bridge was out on the main road from Lone Tree into Hills, and typically Paul Goody did not want to inconvenience the wedding guests by having them drive around. Marilyn remembered that the weather was cold and sleety. Rich had a bad case of the flu, and at one point during the rehearsal he whispered to her a little gamely, "Don't worry if I'm gone for a little bit. I'll be back."

They did not take a honeymoon, which was probably just as well considering that Marilyn came down with Rich's flu a couple of days later. At first the newlyweds rented an apartment in Iowa City, but within a few months they moved out to the farm with Rich's parents. In the spring, Marilyn and Rich would often attend the dances held to benefit local volunteer fire departments. In the winter, they rode their snowmobile for miles over the frozen, snowy fields to visit friends without ever touching a public roadway.

Marilyn worked alongside Rich, driving tractor and working with the hogs. After the Goodys' children were born, they spent a lot of time out on the tractor too. Sometimes Marilyn and Rich would each take a child on their lap as they steered equipment around the fields. Rich and Marilyn shared the domestic chores as well. More than many men, Rich looked after the kids around the house. Not only that, he seemed to enjoy it.

Neighbors noticed that Rich had an affinity for children. He would come in from driving tractor just to play with visiting kids when he saw their parents' car pulled up in the drive. Children around Lone Tree reciprocated, often including him in their games. One family still has a home video of Rich playing with the neighborhood kids, who have dressed him in an absurdly comic collection of ill-fitting pants, coat, and hat.

When Rich was a boy, he had helped his family plant a grove of pines near the confluence of two small creeks at the back of their property. As the years passed, the trees grew to considerable height. The only grove of conifers visible anywhere in that part of Johnson County, the Goodys' woods became a haven for wildlife. They were also where Rich went if he needed to think about something, or just get away by himself.

Now, twenty years later as a father, he brought his children, Rachel and Mark, there and taught them to recognize the tracks of racoon, muskrat, and deer in the soft mud along the edge of the creek. They were quick to absorb his love of the place, as was Marilyn. Sometimes in the fall when Rich was working the fields, Marilyn and Rachel would sit in the long grass along the creek and release milkweed to watch the cotton drift on the wind.

It was around this time that Rich got to know Duane Brun, who rents a farm to the south. "Duane helped Rich loosen up and laugh again," recalled Marilyn. Like Rich, Duane Brun was an inveterate practical joker. Soon the two of them had intricate pranks under way. Duane remembered one time that Rich snuck over to the Bruns' and put all their boots up on the roof. Another time, Duane and some mutual friends snuck over to the Goodys' and put the dual wheels from his tractor in front of the doors to the machine shed.

Early the next morning Duane received a call from Rich. Rich was cordial enough, and even complimented him on rolling the tires fifty yards up the bank. Confronted in this fashion, Duane Brun admitted his culpability. It was only later that he realized that Rich really did not know that Duane was the one. It was just a hunch "until he got me to admit it," Duane Brun said with an appreciative laugh.

When Duane and Donna Brun's younger daughter was born, the Goodys took care of the Bruns' son while Duane rushed Donna to the hospital. Donna Brun remembered it was six o'clock in the morning when Duane called the Goodys to say that her labor pains had begun. "The phone only rang once before Rich picked it up," he said.

Another neighbor, Harold Schuessler, recalled Rich's desire to better himself as a farmer. Harold and Rich used to talk over the fence that separated the Schuessler farm from the Leslie Parizek place, which the Goodys worked as tenants. Chatting about this and that—and nothing in particular, as is the country fashion—they became friends.

Somehow, this sort of friendship never developed with the neighbor on the other side of the Parizeks, Dale Burr. Several factors divided the Burrs and the Goodys, but one dominated the rest. This was the land: specifically, the Leslie Parizek place.

Rich Goody knew the route from his home to the Parizek place as well as he knew his catechism, having learned it by the same method of relentless repetition.

Six miles of section line road separated the Goody home place from the Parizeks', and Rich drove it often. Since the distance between the two farms was short, there was a great deal of ferrying equipment back and forth between the pieces of land.

Rich's normal route carried him on dirt and gravel road, except for crossing X-14 a couple miles north of Lone Tree. Often he would use the old unmaintained section line right-of-way behind the Parizeks' as a shortcut. That way, he did not have to pass directly in front of the Burr house, which guarded the approach to the Parizek place from the south.

Tucked in the fold of the gently undulating prairie, the Parizek farm was beautifully situated. It had a southern exposure, some protection against the north wind, and good drainage. The soil was Tama Dickenson complex loam, one of the richest types in all of Iowa. At the top of the rise sat the Parizek home itself, an imposing white house with a huge porch facing due west toward the sunset.

Although his family had no claim to the property, Rich had seen it at every hour of the day, and had an opportunity to appreciate its many virtues close hand. In time, the land became woven into his memories of growing up, as well as his hopes for the future. Rich could see what was possible with this sweet little eighty-acre parcel if one owned it. And like so many young men before him, he dreamed of owning the piece of land that accepted his sweat.

Rich did not have the financial resources to seriously think about buying the Parizek place, however. In fact, when he first returned from duty in Vietnam, he had trouble borrowing even a little from local banks. Eventually Elmer Draker at the Hills Bank and Trust loaned Rich the money he needed, making him a typically loyal Hills Bank customer, which he remained after John Hughes took over the bank.

Since he could not expand, Rich had no choice but to do the best with what was available to him. This meant that Rich, like his father, sought a level of production that would maximize income over expenses, rather than maximum production per se. While the Burrs might typically fertilize for 180 bushels of corn per acre, the Goodys might fertilize for 140 bushels of corn per acre on the Parizek place next door, figuring that the final 20-plus percent increase in production was not worth the expense.

Although the Burrs' gross income per acre was invariably higher, their expenses were too. As a result, their net income per acre was sometimes less than what the Goodys and Parizeks together earned from identical land on the other side of the one-lane dirt road. The Burrs' big advantage was their freedom from debt. They owned their land free and clear, and for two generations they had not needed to borrow money for operating expenses. This meant that the Burrs got to keep the 10 percent or more that most American farmers lost to the banks as an inescapable cost of doing business. It also helped offset what the Burrs lost to late harvest and inefficiently high production goals.

When Dale Burr took over the family operation from his father in 1974, the Burrs were entirely debt free. Although they no longer controlled their own bank, they still possessed substantial assets in the form of real estate, stocks, and cash. "We thought he [Dale] could write a check for twenty thousand dollars any time he wanted to," observed Bob Berry. Another cousin and neighbor, Leland Stock, said, "We thought everything was looking good [for the Burrs]. You know, money in the bank and farmland sticking out their ears . . . We figured if anybody had the money to buy farmland, they were going to buy it. The rest of us had to go to the banker, see, and do a little begging."

Through the late 1970s, Dale was able to finance the purchase of both equipment and land without having to go see the banker, but this changed by the early 1980s. Dale's appetite for racehorses and his habitual tardiness played a part in his increasing need to borrow, as did the fortunes of his son. Then in his early thirties, John Burr was one of the most aggressive of the boomers then bidding Johnson County farmland to record heights. In 1977, John Burr purchased the eighty-acre Weise place for $140,000, and three years later he purchased the Mueller place for $142,000. As John's purchases continued, he was forced to rely on his father's financial support to swing land deals. Dale signed mortgages for his son and loaned him money outright.

Thus, John was essentially acting as an agent of the larger family when he first entered into discussions about buying the Parizek place in 1982. Leslie Parizek's farm was more attractive to the Burrs than almost any other piece of property in the area because of its location. Acquiring Leslie Parizek's farm would allow them to connect Dale's land with the original home place of John's namesake, John P. Burr. It would also give the Burrs almost all the land in Section 26 except for the holdings of Harold Schuessler. In the games of real-estate checkers that occupy the imaginations of many winter-bound farmers, this was an admirable move. Controlling all—or even a sizable part—of a square-mile section represented a level of achievement that not many attained.

Yet even as the Burrs reached for their dream, there were signs of trouble at home and abroad. In part because of his ambitious pursuit of additional property, John Burr had actually lost money in each of the previous three years. According to his federal income tax statements, he lost approximately $6,000 in 1980, $5,000 in 1981, and $8,000 in

1982 on an average annual gross income of $200,000. There were also indications that American farmers generally were headed for hard times. In the wake of President Jimmy Carter's 1980 embargo on sale of American wheat to the Soviet Union, American agricultural exports began to decline for the first time in a decade. As a result, the government was left holding more and more grain in storage. By the end of 1982, the U.S. government was storing 3.4 billion bushels of surplus corn, or about half a year's crop.

Even more portentous was the fact that 1982 was the first year in a quarter-century that farmland values declined in Iowa. And yet the Burrs still pursued the Parizek place. John Burr believed that land prices were nowhere near their peak. A friend remembers how John predicted that Johnson County farmland would reach $10,000 an acre, more than four times its 1982 price. Friends believe a sort of land mania overcame Dale and John when it came to the Parizek place. "It just gets to the point where nothing matters— friends, your longtime neighbors," said Leland Stock. "They was afraid their neighbor would buy it."

During the summer of 1982, when he learned that Leslie Parizek was seriously interested in selling, John Burr made him an offer many landowners at the time would have found hard to refuse. It was so high, in fact, that the deal was sealed before the property ever hit the open market. In July 1982, John purchased Leslie Parizek's eighty acres, plus the house and outbuildings, for $300,000. He was to pay $60,000 that year ($5,000 down, $10,000 by September 15, 1982, $45,000 by November 15), and $32,000 per year thereafter. This figured out to $3,750 an acre, just about the highest price ever paid for Lincoln Township farmland. The contract further stipulated that Leslie Parizek did not have to notify Rich Goody about the sale: That responsibility fell to the buyer.

If John Burr intended to evict Rich Goody and farm the Parizek place himself in 1983, Iowa law required that he give Goody notice of his intention by September 1, 1982. This was in fact John's plan, but during July and early August he did not get around to it. Then in the latter part of August it became apparent to everyone in the community that Paul Goody was dying. It seemed impossibly rude to tell Rich Goody he was evicted from the Parizek place when his father was mortally ill, and so John held off until after Paul passed away, which was September 1, 1982. Two more weeks went by, and then on September 17 (two days after he had to make his second payment to Leslie Parizek) John Burr went into the bank to talk about a loan. While there, he learned that Rich planned to farm the Parizek place again in 1983. That night John stopped by the Goody place to talk to Rich.

It did not go well. The best the two old schoolmates could agree on was that they would have to talk again soon, but even then there was a misunderstanding. John Burr thought Rich Goody was going to come see him; Rich Goody thought the opposite. Two more weeks passed before John finally did go see Rich again on October 5. He found Rich working on his combine and did not mince his words. With the kind of debt load he had taken on, John needed to maximize his profits, and that meant farming the Parizek place himself. He was sorry, he said, but he owned the land, and there just was no room in the picture anymore for Rich Goody. John's manner was brusque and matter-of-fact, but if he expected Rich to acquiesce any faster this time because his claim was more bluntly stated, he was wrong.

Rich knew his rights and stated them plainly. Iowa law required that evicted farm tenants be notified by "restricted certified mail" before September 1. He had not been notified. Therefore he said he was certain he would be farming the Parizek place in 1983, unless John wanted to buy him out. Recounting his own reaction, John Burr said, "I mentioned he was out of line and abusing the law 'trying to see what he could get,' when he said I could buy him out. Furthermore I stated my intention of grazing stalks after harvest. And yes, before leaving I told Goody that I would not tolerate his trying to farm the place another year." If he persisted in his effort to farm the Parizek place, John said he could make it difficult for Rich.

Still Rich Goody held his ground. If anything, John Burr's not-so-veiled threat increased his determination, for Rich was no less proud than John. "They were so much alike, yet such different people," a mutual friend recalled. While John was one of the most prominent bachelors around, Rich was a family man who had married young and put a lot of his energy into raising his kids. While John Burr had attended two universities, Rich had gone no further in school than Lone Tree High School. Rich had seen battle duty in Vietnam, while John had never been to war. It was as difficult to picture Rich Goody with a coterie of Cedar Rapids attorneys as it was to imagine John Burr as an usher at St. Joseph's Catholic Church in Hills. Both were completely devoted to farming—especially hog farming—but their situations made them natural antagonists.

For John, Rich was a person who stood in the way of his taking possession of land he wanted badly, and that had cost him dearly. For Rich, John was one of the big operators who were gobbling up smaller farmers, and making matters particularly difficult for tenants by driving up land prices and rents (just as they had during the World War I boom). It also must have galled Rich to realize that although his hog operation might be more efficient than John's, John was likely to win out simply because he was bigger and his family had greater financial leverage.

Why, he must have asked himself, should I politely step aside for a guy who is putting a nail in my coffin? Jay Honohan, Rich's attorney, confirmed his belief that he need not step aside. Honohan told the Goodys he was confident that they either would be able to farm the Parizek place the next year or would win a monetary settlement from the Burrs. Legally, the case seemed cut and dried, but in terms of community mores it was not. Paul Goody's death had legitimately complicated the notification period for eviction. There was also a sort of unwritten understanding that you did not sue a person over late notification, at least not if you ever intended to see the defendant at the café, or bank, or ball game.

Rich was mad, and more than a little concerned about what the future might bring for his family, farming an even smaller place in a world where only the big fish survived. While authorizing Honohan to take legal action, he expressed concern that John Burr might make good on his threat immediately. On October 11, Honohan therefore wrote to John Burr: "You told Rich that you wanted to turn cattle and hogs loose in the fields. You may not do this without his permission . . . Also you told him 'you would make it hard for him to farm if he doesn't give up the place.' Any trouble that you give the Goodys could be the source of a damage claim against you in a lawsuit."

Shortly after receiving Honohan's letter, which he termed "harassment," John Burr took action. At night, when he knew Rich would be at home, he drove his big Steiger tractor across the road and chisel plowed all the tillable land on the Parizek place, rendering the fields useless to anyone until spring.

9

On December 6, 1982, Richard and Marilyn Goody sued John Burr in Iowa District Court. Alleging that they had been illegally evicted from the Parizek place, the Goodys sought $8,000, which they estimated the land would have earned them in 1983. In addition, they asked for $100,000 in punitive damages for the threats and "malicious" actions of John Burr.

The Goodys' attorney, Jay Honohan, was one of the leading lawyers in the area. A former city attorney of Iowa City, he had also represented the City of Hills in the rail-road right-of-way annexation deal. A $100,000 punitive damages claim by him had to be taken seriously, as soon became evident. In September 1983, Iowa District Judge L. Vern Robinson handed down a summary judgment in favor of the Goodys.

On the facts of the case, there was little to argue. Iowa law had required something like September 1 notification of evictions since 1860 as a means of bringing order to agricultural rents. The Iowa State Supreme Court had repeatedly upheld the constitutionality of the notification law, and most farmers were frankly aware of it. In the eyes of the court, the only thing to be decided was the amount of damages to be awarded the Goodys.

When that portion of the case came to trial in early 1984, John Burr's attorney, Russell Newell, maintained that the Burrs owed the Goodys nothing. Newell argued that even if Rich had been involved, John Burr would have insisted on operating the farm in the manner he actually followed while working it himself in 1983. That year, instead of the heavy soybean crop the Goodys had planted on the Parizek place previously, John Burr planted it entirely to corn. In retrospect, it is obvious that soybeans were the crop to have chosen that year. As a result, John Burr lost money on the Parizek place the first year he farmed it, and he claimed the Goodys would have lost money too.

Honohan replied vehemently that Rich Goody should not be penalized because John Burr's farm judgment proved worse that Rich's. "Defendant [John Burr] attempts to impose his more expensive habits on the plaintiff," he told Iowa District Judge William L. Thomas. Honohan pushed the punitive damage claim aggressively. "Defendant has disregarded the Goodys, the Goodys' lawyer's advice, his own lawyer's advice, and then in 1983 he ignores Discovery Interrogatories [asking for exact corn yield figures, instead of estimated wagonloads]. . . . Despite all the warnings and admonitions, defendant engaged in [behavior] that could lead to violence. Suppose Goody had come on the farm at the time the plowing was done. A fight could easily have started."

Despite the heated nature of some of the courtroom exchanges, Judge Thomas steadfastly refused to become emotionally embroiled in the conflict between the two families. His ruling, handed down on March 6, 1984, was suffused with the cool spirit of compromise. He awarded the Goodys $5,829.60 in compensation for lost income, or roughly a quarter less than they requested. On the much more financially serious question of punitive damages, the judge denied the Goodys' claim. Nine months later, on December 27, 1984, Rich Goody received a check from John Burr for $6,626.96, including interest. This closed the matter in the eyes of the law, but it hardly put it to rest around Hills and Lone Tree. "There was definitely bad blood there," observed a neighbor.

One reason the bitterness remained was that both families suffered from the deterioration of the American farm economy during the early 1980s. American farmers were, in fact, headed toward their first full-scale crash since the Great Depression, when federal controls on agricultural production were instituted for the first time as a part of the New Deal. Although relaxed during World War II and subsequently diluted by more conservative administrations, the basic New Deal system of allotments and subsidies effectively blunted the historic twenty-year cycle of boom and bust in American agriculture until it was dismantled by President Richard Nixon.

Nixon had so little interest in agriculture that he proposed the abolition of the Department of Agriculture in March 1971. Rebuffed by Congress, Nixon appointed a new director of the Department of Agriculture whose policies seemed designed to accomplish much of the President's original aim. The former Dean of Agriculture at Purdue University and board member of three Fortune 500 corporations (including Ralston Purina), Earl Butz wanted to reduce government regulation, or as he liked to put it, "get the government off the farmer's back." A powerful personality and the most effective Secretary of Agriculture since Henry A. Wallace, Butz used the lure of immediate agricultural export profits to convince Congress and many American farmers that production controls were no longer needed. With passage of the Agriculture and Consumer Protection Act of 1973, American farmers were, for the most part, free to grow as much as they wanted, and free from government support.

Most Midwestern farmers—the Burrs and Goodys included—responded by increasing production of corn and soybeans, and initially the results were salubrious. As crop failures hit much of the world, including rich agricultural areas of the Soviet Union, American farmers sold ever-increasing amounts of food on the world market at good prices. Encouraged by Butz, who urged farmers to "plant fencerow to fencerow," agriculture boomed. Farm incomes rose while the cost of government farm support dropped. It appeared that the Nixon Administration had accomplished two goals that had been mutually exclusive for decades.

Rampant inflation helped convince many farmers that they were better off borrowing and buying today than sitting and waiting. The election of President Ronald Reagan, however, marked a weather change on this front. The worst crashes in American agricultural history—1819, 1837, 1857, 1873, 1893, 1920—all occurred when a prolonged period of inflation was followed by rapid deflation. In an unmanaged economy of the sort that Nixon and Reagan strove to reintroduce, this was a prescription for a crash. Yet this was exactly what Republican farm leaders like Senator Jesse Helms and Secretary of Agriculture John Block sought during the early 1980s. Cut loose from the anchor of governmental production controls that had long restrained the fundamental tendencies of the free market, the American agricultural economy responded once again to the tidelike cycles of boom and bust. Having floated up with the flood, it now came down hard on its keel, harder than it had for a half-century.

Ironically, the trigger proved to be the decline in American agricultural exports that followed President Carter's 1980 Soviet grain embargo. Between 1981 and 1983, American agricultural exports fell 12 percent. For an agriculture that lived or died by export sales, this was very bad news. By 1982, estimates for net farm income had dropped so low that the U.S. Department of Agriculture stopped publishing them for a time. One reason for the department's action was the fear that figures for net farm income might cause undue alarm: Adjusted for the effects of inflation, they were lower than during the Depression. In February 1985, the entire South Dakota state legislature went to Washington, D.C., to lobby Congress for farm aid. At House agriculture subcommittee hearings that month, Rep. Steve Gunderson of Wisconsin said, "Clearly, with the credit crisis confronting agriculture, we are literally facing the fundamental destruction of rural society."

Although court decisions delayed federal farm agencies under Ronald Reagan from carrying out the large-scale foreclosures they desired, private banks were under no such restraint. As the crisis deepened, they began to foreclose on farmers all over the country. Even so, many banks heavily involved in agricultural loans were themselves jeopardized. About fifty federally insured agricultural banks failed during 1985, and many more were in danger. At the end of 1985, Iowa Banking Superintendent William Bernau said that 150 of the state's 511 banks had "abnormal loan problems," meaning that questionable loans make up 60 percent or more of their capital base. "Any bank that has abnormal problem loans will have a natural shyness about making a loan to marginal, or problem, borrowers," Bernau said. "If the customer has past due loans, or won't cash flow, the banker would be well advised to say no."

Family farmers were most frequently caught in the credit vise, and among them the ones hurt worst were the boomers, the "progressive" farmers who had borrowed heavily for land and equipment purchases during the late 1970s and early 1980s. Thirty months before, they had been considered among the most successful farmers in their communities, living examples of what a man could accomplish with his own hands if he was willing to work hard and borrow even harder. Now thousands of them found themselves facing financial ruin. Explaining how this could be, one farmer told Congress, which was considering a new farm bill, "If you go to Iowa and have to pay three thousand five hundred dollars an acre for land, there is no way you can raise enough corn or beans on that land to make it pay for itself, assuming twelve percent interest. You just cannot do it."

This is exactly the position in which John Burr found himself. He had paid more than $3,500 an acre for the Parizek place, with 13 percent interest and annual payments of $32,000. Court records show that the property was hard-pressed to gross $16,000 a year in 1983. This meant that John had to pay at least $16,000 out of pocket to the bank for the privilege of farming the Parizek place. He also had land payments due on the other parcels he farmed. For instance, he rented land and buildings from his grandmother for approximately $10,000 a year, but had not paid her in two years. Hilda Burr unknowingly loaned John more than $30,000 in 1984 and 1985. Dale too had loaned more than $60,000 to his son, including the pivotal $40,000 he borrowed for him from the Hills Bank.

As the pressure built on John Burr during the spring of 1985, his hog operation was hit by one of the difficulties of scale that frequently accompany the economies of scale on large specialized farms, namely disease. In intensive modern livestock operations, the difficulty in achieving a perfect balance of feed, space, ventilation, and manure disposal at all times can result in a variety of disease problems. The same diseases were present in old-fashioned operations, but the crowding common in large-scale livestock production increases the threat of epidemic. This is what happened in March 1985, when John lost five hundred hogs, or roughly one quarter his yearly production, to a disease known as TGE.

At that time, John Burr owned or rented 360 acres of prime Johnson County farmland, with a total debt of more than $500,000. This debt was secured with loans on the land he and Dale farmed, but the value of the land was declining almost daily. By late 1985, farmland prices had fallen so steeply that John's net worth was approaching zero. He was grossing nearly a quarter of a million dollars a year, and yet he was on the edge of losing it all. No matter how hard he worked, the land would not pay the debt service, let alone other expenses or an income to him.

John's principal ally and chief supporter in all of his trouble was Dale. The elder Burr not only loved his son, he was almost awed by him: his education, his high spirits, his good looks. John was the shining future, and Dale would do anything to protect him, even though he knew that his son's impetuousness had caused them both difficulties.

"I can't control what John does," he admitted to a friend once after loaning his son money.

As John's financial distress widened to include Dale, the elder Burr became increasingly bitter about the Goodys' lawsuit. More than John, he nourished a personal grievance against Rich Goody.

Perhaps Dale took the Goody lawsuit harder than his son because he was the one who ultimately paid for the settlement, as the money Dale gave John over the 1984 holidays indicates.

Dale also had shouldered a crippling share of the risk. Because he had pledged a significant amount of his own property as collateral for land purchases made in John's name, Dale stood to lose at least as much as his son if the deals went bad and ended in foreclosure.

Still, the court-ordered settlement with Rich Goody was a small, almost inconsequential portion of the Burrs' snowballing debt problem. Why did Dale focus on a $6,000 loss when he and John both owed others much more? What made this small altercation loom as large in his mind as the high-stakes difficulties he was having with the Hills Bank?

A partial explanation may be found in Dale's youth, and the feeling of community he developed growing up around Lone Tree. Unlike his son, Dale was the product of an older cooperative agrarian culture. Before the tractor, survival often hinged on help from surrounding farmsteads, and the value of a farm was judged by the quality of both its soil and neighbors. Without the assistance of neighbors, a farmer might not be able to get his crops in the barn.

Working side by side through the seasons, farmers saw their neighbors under pressure and got to know what kind of person they really were. The same was true of the farm wives who gathered in steamy kitchens to cook for the large migrant farm-work crews. Although sometimes stiflingly provincial, American farm communities at their best were exceptionally strong and resilient, almost like an extended family.

This began to change with the mechanization of American farming. Henry A. Wallace observed people being "tractored off" the land as early as 1939, but the real impact of mechanization was not felt until after World War II. Nineteen fifty-four was the first year that the number of tractors exceeded the number of horses and mules on American farms. And tractors were just the beginning. Mechanical harvesters for potatoes, onions, almonds, green peas, cucumbers, and tomatoes were among the many new implements developed.

Perhaps even more significant were the tremendous increases in the application of artificial fertilizers and chemicals. Commercial fertilizer was used in the Midwest in the early years of the twentieth century, but it was not until the 1930s that it was applied to corn. World War II started a trend toward heavier use of artificial fertilizers that accelerated during the 1950s and 1960s. In fact, the continuing growth in American farm production during these decades was probably due to escalating fertilizer use more than anything else. While the use of power machinery increased 30 percent between 1950 and 1970, the use of artificial fertilizer increased by 276 percent.

Still further increases in production were obtained through advances in breeding. The principle of hybrid vigor, discovered in 1917 by Donald Jones of Illinois's Funk Seeds, proved to be one of the most fruitful agricultural innovations of the twentieth century. Crossing two corn plants that were themselves the progeny of self-pollinated plants, Jones observed a remarkable one-generation increase in size, vigor, and regularity. Like so many of the newer plant varieties, hybrid corn was ideally suited to large-scale cultivation. By the late 1940s, it was possible to drive all day through Iowa without ever seeing anything but hybrid corn.

Hybrid seed made it possible for farmers to double their yield, but it cost more. Since the seed would not breed true, it had to be purchased new every year. Improved livestock breeds similarly increased the production of such staples as milk, but purebred animals were more expensive than the mixed-stock animals they replaced. Tractors and fertilizer further boosted the basic out-of-pocket expense of operating a farm, not to mention the investment necessary to get in the game. According to the U.S. Department of Agriculture, in 1930 an average investment of less than $5,000 was associated with each American farm laborer. By 1958, that total had more than tripled, to $18,000.

To meet these increasing expenses, farmers borrowed. In 1920, $5,000 was a large loan. By the 1950s, loans four times that size were becoming commonplace. The indebtedness of Iowa farmers increased every year during the period 1950–55, and then really took off the next year when Congress liberalized important government agricultural loan programs. Not only were larger loans authorized, but revisions permitted broader use of federal loans to refinance both secured and unsecured debts. The period from July 1, 1956, through June 30, 1957, was the heaviest loan-writing period in the history of the Farmers Home Administration to that point.

With American farm production growing by almost 5 percent annually, the price of farm produce generally failed to keep pace with the increasing price of farmland, or virtually anything else. As a result, the administration of President Dwight Eisenhower was forced somewhat reluctantly to curtail production. While programs like the Soil Bank, which paid farmers to take land out of production, were successful in preventing a major crash, they could not entirely overcome the agricultural glut. Farm prices were soft in the late 1950s, and land prices sagged temporarily. As before, the only way for farmers to make more money on a declining margin was to grow more. And so even though the larger mechanized farmers were at the root of the problem, smaller farms failed at the highest rate.

By 1950, small farmers were also beginning to be hurt by some of the New Deal programs that were originally intended to help them, such as the large Western public irrigation projects. Denied the public subsidies that flowed to users of public irrigation (which supplied water at less than cost), thousands of farmers in older agricultural areas found themselves being forced down by an unseen hand: the subsidy they paid through taxes to their competitors. Apples from Washington's Columbia River Basin put orchardists out of business all over the United States, just as lettuce and other fresh produce from California's Imperial Valley put truck farmers out of business from coast to coast.

During the New Deal people were led to believe that the new irrigated lands would go to farmers who were victims of the Dust Bowl, but after Roosevelt's death federal policy encouraged the flow of irrigation benefits to corporations rather than small farmers. Later administrations ignored federal law limiting recipients of federal irrigation to 160 acres of irrigated land, thereby allowing large tracts of the best Western land to come under the control of food conglomerates. At the same time, vertically integrated corporate control became prevalent in poultry farming as the small independents were driven out by large national poultry feed suppliers like Ralston Purina Corp.

According to a 1959 California House of Representatives report on the corporate takeover of that state's poultry industry, the feed companies encouraged overproduction, then "simply stated the price they wanted to pay . . . to force the poultrymen out of business or into an integrated setup." This move toward vertical integration was extremely attractive to the feed corporations, since it put them in a position to extract maximum profit from both the sale of feed at the outset and the sale of the finished poultry "product" at the end of the process. For the poultry farmers who actually did the work of raising the millions of birds involved, however, it was disastrous. Consumption (and thus work) rose, but the farmer's pay declined in some cases to less an hour than the supermarket checker who sold the chicken.

Iowa farmers were not affected as much as some, partly because they were not that heavily involved with poultry on a commercial basis, and partly because they blocked vertical integration of the beef industry with state laws. Iowa farmers also received water subsidies (during the 1950s, the federal government helped pay for construction of ten thousand stock-watering ponds and ten thousand wells in Iowa). Yet even in favored agricultural locales like the Midwest, there was less opportunity for the young, either to own their own farm or to work on someone else's place. Farm employment declined more than one third during the 1950s and early 1960s alone as an average of nearly a million Americans left the farm annually.

Part of what the *Washington Post* described in 1971 as "the greatest migration in history," these people brought to 40 million the total number driven off American farms since World War I. Like the English yeoman farmers who were enclosed during Tudor times four hundred years before, most of the dispossessed farm population ended up as urban wage workers: During the 1950s, nearly 40 percent of the growth in the nonagricultural labor force came from people getting out of agriculture. As Wendell Berry noted in *The Unsettling of America,* "Here surely is cause for mourning: a forced migration of people greater than any in history, the foretelling of riots in the cities, and the failure of human community in the country."

More than a simple loss of people, the depopulation of rural America meant fundamental changes in rural communities. Thanks to the automobile and telephone, it was easier than ever for people to get together, but people actually saw each other less, and in less meaningful circumstances. "As soon as it became technologically possible to farm independently, everybody wanted that," observed Pastor James Schutter of the United Methodist Church in Tingley, Iowa. "Machines made you really self-reliant. People didn't realize that machines would also make you isolated." Recalled another old-time Iowa farmer, "There used to be a country school here. We'd have community dinners. We'd get together and thrash and have dinner, but we don't do it anymore."

Now men essentially employ money and machinery, instead of people, to do their work for them. The incessant, age-old agricultural struggle is becoming increasingly impersonal. Like high-tech soldiers, many of today's farmers have become isolated from the human dimension of what they do. Dale Burr was entirely capable of farming without the assistance of friends like the Bulines and Schuesslers, let alone casual acquaintances like the Goodys. In a very literal sense of the expression, the Burrs did not need the Goodys, and the reverse was equally true.

Although united in their opposition to the Goodys, Dale's and John's attitudes were different. The younger Burr was furious at Rich Goody, but he did not feel betrayed. A child of the tractor era, John Burr understood that the fundamental tenet of modern farm economics is every man for himself. Dale, however, carried within him the code of the older era.

It hardly mattered that Dale and his family had done much more than Rich Goody to destroy the old farm community. Dale saw Rich Goody's lawsuit over the Parizek place as a clear affront to the values of his youth. The dollar amount didn't matter either. To Dale, it was the principle of the thing.

It was a little after ten-thirty on the morning of December 9, 1985, when Marilyn Goody and her son, Mark, climbed into the family pickup. The packed snow on the Goody drive was exceptionally slippery, but Marilyn maneuvered the four-wheel-drive Ford out onto the section line road with ease.

Although she was a small, sparrowlike woman, Marilyn Goody was capable of driving a tractor or combine, as well as keeping a tidy house. Rachel, the Goodys' nine-year-old daughter, was in school that morning, and by taking Mark with her, Marilyn freed Rich to work in the fields, where he had been hauling manure.

She intended to go to the Hills Bank and then do a little grocery shopping at Casey's Store. Mark, who had just turned six the week before, played on the rocking horses the Hills Bank had placed in a corner, and then campaigned for a treat when they went across the street to the store. Everyone said Mark reminded them of Rich more and more all the time.

Back on the snowy streets, Marilyn noted that Dale Burr's pickup was parked in the lot behind the Hills Bank. Seeing it gave her a pang, but like the rest of the Goodys, she thought they had put the whole unpleasant experience with the Burrs behind them at that point. The last couple of days, in particular, had been good ones for the Goody family.

On Saturday night they had attended mass at St. Joseph's Church in Hills because Rich was afraid of the weather forecast and didn't want to miss church as they had the previous Sunday. The weather was not unusually cold for Johnson County, Iowa, at that time of the year, but there had been a threat of meanness in the gathering gray clouds Saturday afternoon.

The feeling was reenforced by the top story on all Iowa newscasts that evening. In the climax of a "bad blood" feud between two neighboring farm families, elderly Nodaway Township farmer Stanley Schenk, sixty, had murdered his neighbor, Louis Davies, thirty-five. Schenk thought Davies was stealing his cows and breaking down his fences. He sued him twice, but did not get satisfaction until the December day when he shot him dead.

The weather held off on Sunday, December 8, and so Rich, his mother, Wilma, and Mark bundled up for the traditional annual trek to get a Christmas tree. They cut a tree together in the pine grove Rich had helped plant at the back of the place as a child, and then carried it home to the little white frame farmhouse with hand-made holiday decorations in the window.

That same evening, the Goodys went to the Lone Tree

School Christmas pageant. Wanda Anderson, Rachel's teacher, remembers that Rich and Marilyn came early, and Rich remarked that he "wouldn't miss it for the world." Rachel and Mark had small parts in the show, and it was obvious to friends that Rich was immensely proud of them both.

When the weather still refused to declare itself the next day, Rich and Marilyn carried on with business as usual. Rich went to work on the place, while Marilyn had several errands to run in Hills. By the time she was finished, it was time to prepare lunch for the family, so she and Mark drove home. Five minutes later, when they turned into the Goodys' drive, Marilyn noticed the same truck she had seen in town—the truck she knew belonged to Dale Burr—parked around the corner to the left by the Goodys' machine shed. Drawing closer, she saw her husband standing face-to-face with Dale Burr.

The pickup's approach seemed to break a spell between the two men, for Rich immediately turned and started to walk away. Dale turned away too and opened up the door of his truck. Reaching in across the seat, he pulled out the old model 31 and raised it. Marilyn had caught him by surprise, and now he was faced with the closest thing to a fair fight he had seen since his errand of death began three-quarters of an hour earlier. Rich was young, in good shape, and on his own turf. If he chose to flee, or had even an instant to seize the initiative, Dale would almost certainly be unable to execute his plan. Furthermore, if Dale did not do something immediately, Rich would be on the other side of the tractor and out of range.

Dale called out to Rich. No one will ever know exactly what he said, but the taunt was effective enough to stop Rich in his tracks and spin him around to face his adversary. It was at that precise instant, with Marilyn and Mark drawing close enough to see what was happening, that Dale shot Rich Goody full in the face from a distance of fifteen feet. Rich's left cheek was torn off and his teeth and jaw were shattered, while other pellets penetrated his eye sockets into the front portion of the brain. The wound was obviously fatal, but Rich Goody did not die immediately. He turned away again, desperately, hopelessly, toward the barn with his right glove still clutched in his hand. Dale then shot him again in the buttocks as he fell face forward in the dirt near the hog feeders, where he lay like a slaughtered animal with his tongue lolling out the gaping cavity where his face had been.

Marilyn instantly threw Mark to the floor of the truck and swung across the snowy yard and garden toward the road. Dale turned and fired the last shot in his magazine at them as they roared away. Several pellets struck the truck's tailgate, but neither Marilyn nor Mark was injured. After plowing through the snow-filled drainage ditch to the road, she swung around and sped north toward Cecil Smith's farm. Several long seconds later, she glanced anxiously in her rearview mirror and saw Dale's truck heading in the opposite direction.

PART FOUR

The land belongs to the future.
Willa Cather

10

When Dale Burr was growing up, the men in the family liked to tell stories about hog drive days. It used to be that farmers around Lone Tree drove their hogs to market like cattle on the Western range. In the fall, they would round up a large group of hogs and set out with them for the stockyards in Iowa City.

Controlling the animals was always a little dicey, especially when crossing a creek bottom. The hogs wanted to wallow in the moist soil, but the farmers used bullwhips and dogs to keep them moving. Closer to town, there was the danger that the hogs would get into gardens and lawns. The farmers worked hard to prevent this, though, as did the prudent homeowners who dropped everything else to guard their property.

You could not accuse a hog drive of sneaking up on anyone. The crack of the whips, the shouting of the men, the bark of the dogs and hogs all told of its approach. It usually took the better part of a hard day to drive the hogs twenty-five miles, but Johnson County farmers counted themselves lucky in the bargain since it let them deliver their animals to Iowa City without having to pay hauling costs. In the early days, farmers used to spend the night in town at the end of the drive, but after the advent of the automobile it became common to bring along a car so that they could motor home.

Of course, things never went exactly as expected. One time a group of farmers from down toward Lone Tree got started with their hogs a little late in the day. They were delayed further along the way so that at dusk they were still miles from Iowa City. The farmers held a quick consultation, and decided they had no choice but to keep moving since they could not camp overnight with a hundred hogs in the middle of the road. One man suggested they use their Ford Model T to light the way. So they steered the car behind the hogs and turned on the headlights.

Instead of moving forward along the lighted road, however, the hogs wheeled around and charged at the car's headlights. The driver was uninjured, but in the mass jostling that ensued, the car's starter crank was broken. Finally, with total darkness on them, the farmers maneuvered the car around in front of the herd of hogs. Again they turned on the lights. Again the hogs moved toward the bright glare. Then the driver threw the car in reverse. They had to back up for miles, but the hogs happily followed the lights all the way to the slaughterhouse door.

This story always drew a good laugh among Dale and his cousins. They instinctively appreciated the way it embarrassed august friends and relatives without causing any really serious harm. There was another dimension too. Like so many good farm yarns, the saga of the hog drive served to illustrate an unexpected deeper principle drawn from homey detail. The men never said it in so many words, but the boys understood that sometimes you cannot approach your goal directly; you have to back into it. The idea stuck with Dale, and seemed to be reflected in his tactics on the morning of December 9.

With both John Hughes and Richard Goody, Dale engaged his victims obliquely. At the bank, Dale talked to a subordinate, went out and bought ammunition, reentered the back door, and pulled out his gun while Hughes's back was turned. With Rich Goody, he also approached the back way, stopping en route to make sure he would be able to kill again, and finally going for his gun when the other man's back was turned. Although he was interrupted at the Goodys', there was evidence there too of the almost ceremonial manner in which he had staged his final encounter with the banker.

Dale did not kill Rich Goody at first any more than he killed Roger Reilly outright when he refused to cash the five-hundred-dollar check. Instead he preferred to toy with his unwitting victims. It was almost as if Dale was giving the Hills Bank and Rich Goody each one last chance to redeem themselves for what he saw as their betrayal of him. In this sub-rosa trial of the accused, Dale played the lamb, giving his victims no reason for suspicion, or cause for holding him at blame. It was only later that he would reveal himself as an avenging angel, sitting in eternal judgment on those who had smitten him. At the bank, the kiss of death occurred when Dale paid Reilly cash for the overdraft on his checking account.

Testing his tormentors must have been tremendously satisfying for Dale. In his mind it gave him a feeling of control, of pulling the strings behind the scenes. Coming on the heels of so many stressful months, it must have also given him an exhilarating sense of freedom. When he stepped into Roger Reilly's office the first time that morning, he was already freed from the concerns that had given the bank its power over him. With his wife, Emily, lying dead on the kitchen floor at home, he no longer had to worry about whether he would be able to farm next year, or where he would get seed money. Like terminal illness, inextricable financial distress had simplified Dale's desires. Now he wanted only one thing: control over the end.

To Dale, power was synonymous with dignity, which was perhaps the most valuable thing he had lost. Yet Dale also wanted something more. He wanted vengeance. The most striking thing about his murder of Emily, John Hughes, and Rich Goody is the vicious, disfiguring violence of the acts. They testify to the fury that drove him, as well as his fundamental belief that others were to blame for his difficulties. In his own mind, it appears Dale saw himself as the aggrieved. All his life he had tried to do things the right way. He had been a good son, a good farmer, a good husband, a good father. What—he might have asked—was his greatest fault? Loving his son too much? Caring too much for the land? Believing too much of what the bankers told him?

Each of these qualities had long been a virtue for Dale. Pheasant hunters brought him offerings because of the corn he left standing, and kids in Lone Tree still benefited from the effort he put into founding the Prairie Masters 4-H chapter. For years, Dale had prospered by trusting his banker father to handle many of the financial decisions involved in the Burrs' large and complex farm enterprise. After Vernon's death, however, Dale reaped more ill than good from what were by then thoroughly ingrained tendencies. With the pheasants gone, people murmured that the corn he left standing maybe meant the old man could not handle the farm anymore. His financial backing of his son—tendered with "love and affection"—cost him more than he ever dreamed and drove him to borrowing. Then, when he trusted John Hughes, the banker began moving to foreclose on him within three months of signing a thirty-year mortgage.

As a farmer, Dale had spent the largest part of his life on the Johnson County land where he worked and lived. He knew every acre of the Burrs' holdings in every kind of weather. All his energy and imagination had been channeled into that land, the task of taking better care of it, and the desire to pass the farm on to his son. "They toiled and suffered," as a nineteenth-century observer noted of American farmers generally, "so that their children might inherit the promise." In Dale's mind there was no excuse for failing this fundamental responsibility. It was a shame that made murder pale by comparison.

In his deepening confusion and anger, Dale was as isolated as the elm that gave Lone Tree its name. He could not go to friends with his difficulties because his self-esteem was inextricably bound up with the ideal of independent self-reliance. With the pride of the Burrs, the last thing he wanted was his neighbors to know he was hurting. And since he had virtually no experience with the world beyond rural Johnson County, he had no sense of how—or even where—to go for help outside the community. The only political farm group that he belonged to was the Farm Bureau, which has worked against concerted political action by farmers (perhaps because impotent uncertainty creates the best climate for selling insurance, which is one of the organization's principal businesses). So without any social or political outlet for his anger, the pressure growing within Dale took a purely personal form of release.

Dale blamed the people around him for his own failure, and each of the murders punctuated what was for him a separate saga of betrayal. Some of the Burrs' friends later speculated that Dale killed his wife to protect her from the embarrassment of financial ruin. It is hard to see brutal murder as an act of kindness and consideration, however, especially considering their increasingly tense relationship. Emily the banker's daughter was already publicly questioning Dale's ability as a provider. She had been the emotional center of Dale's life for nearly forty years. Her condemnation—real or imagined—would have been the cruelest cut of all. Any of several little things could have set Dale off that morning, and once he had killed her he was beyond the point of no return. His hours were numbered, but he still had enough time to attend to a couple of important matters.

As Dale drove south from the Goody place, he rolled down the window on his truck all the way. The chill December air filled the cab and sent it dancing with tiny particles of ice as he followed the gravel section line road south. Dale waved to a casual friend, Donna Brun, as he passed the first farm on the left and continued on toward the farm of distant relative Kenneth Musser. Mrs. J. D. Musser was an acknowledged expert on Burr family history who had composed an ode to the Lone Tree elm shortly before the historic tree's death. The poem concluded:

> It stands restored, and not alone;
> As in the days of old,
> And of its help to pioneer,
> many a story is told.

Did Dale wonder what stories would be told about him and his solitary stand? Or was he still too intent on his plan for personal justice to ponder the judgment of history?

Certainly, more and more people were wondering what Dale planned with every passing minute. At 11:24 A.M. that morning, when the call came in reporting that John Hughes had been shot, Johnson County Sheriff's Lieutenant Robert Carpenter dispatched Deputy David Henderson to the Farmers and Merchants Bank in Lone Tree in case this was Dale's next target. Apprised of the situation, Farmers and Merchants officials decided to close the bank. With Dale still at large, law-enforcement officers began warning other banks in the region that they might be in danger. Based on hasty consultations between the first law-enforcement officers to arrive in Hills and bank officials there, a preliminary list of others who might be targets of Dale's was compiled. Then it had to be radically expanded when the call came in from Marilyn Goody reporting that Dale Burr had just murdered her husband.

The authorities suddenly realized that if Dale was willing to kill over his grievances against people like John Hughes and Rich Goody, there was no telling whom he might have in mind next. The bankers he dealt with at the Farmers and Merchants and Columbus Junction banks were two obvious potential targets. Others near the top of the list were Tim Smith from the Hills Bank, Leslie Parizek, certain personnel in the ASCS and Cedar-Johnson Farm Supply offices, and possibly neighbors and members of the Hills Bank's board of directors. As the calls went out and the news of Dale's rampage began to spread through the Johnson County grapevine, more than a few people thought back on recent encounters with Dale with a new keenness, reflecting if they might have given cause for a maniac to kill.

At that moment, Dale was continuing south into one of the more deserted parts of Pleasant Valley Township. At the bottom of a slight grade, he came to a sign warning BRIDGE OUT. Beside it stood an old windmill that had been disconnected so that its turning blades no longer pumped water. It was heavily rusted, but the name of its manufacturer —The Aermotor of Chicago—was still legible. There were no houses nearby, and since the bridge was washed out, little traffic passed by. It was not unusual to see a hawk seize a snake here, soar up over the road with the serpent writhing in its beak, and then come down in the next cornfield to consume its prey. In season, meadowlarks sang from twisted old fence posts, and pheasants skulked in the brakes.

Dale turned left and followed the creek east for a couple of miles. Near a group of A-frame hog houses and a NO HUNTING sign, he turned again. Heading south one mile, he purposefully jogged left once more, so that he passed cousin Wayne Burr's place. A few hundred yards more and he started up the slight rise to the intersection where the section line road met X-14. From here, he could turn right, toward Lone Tree, or keep going to Columbus Junction. If he turned left, he could double back to Hills. If he went straight and continued across X-14, he could strike another target near his home.

Dale had come to the moment of decision. He was no longer fleeing the Goodys. He was headed somewhere else. And at exactly that moment, Deputy Sheriff David Henderson flew over the rise on X-14 and spotted Dale just as he was slowing to a stop at the intersection.

Although Henderson was in a hurry as he sped north out of Lone Tree that morning, he was not looking forward to encountering his quarry. A minute or two before, the police radio had notified him that Dale Burr had shot Rich Goody.

Henderson had been at the bank in Lone Tree when it locked its doors. He knew Dale had been there several times during the last ten days trying to borrow money and had been turned down. Leaving a deputy from nearby Nichols posted on guard, Henderson proceeded north to try to intercept Dale.

A good-looking, clean-shaven man in his early thirties, Henderson was alone in an unmarked beige patrol car with grill lights and a cherry on the dash. He had all his lights on—but not his siren—as he opened it up heading north on X-14. He had not even gotten up top speed, however, when he saw a green and white GMC pickup coming in on a section line road only a mile north of Lone Tree. It matched the description of Dale's truck.

Dale pulled across X-14 in front of the patrol car, and for an instant before he accelerated away on the snowy section line road, the deputy saw the farmer's emotionless face. As soon as Henderson pulled in behind Dale's truck, he knew he had found their man. Turning off his lights, he followed Burr east on the unnamed section line road and reported his position to the Johnson County Sheriff's Department by radio. Dale was not driving too rapidly—perhaps forty to forty-five miles per hour—but he was steadily leading Henderson deeper into the unpaved backroads of rural Johnson County in an area Dale knew well. In addition, Henderson realized they were within a couple of miles of the Muscatine/ Johnson County line.

Adding still more pressure to the situation was the fact that Johnson County Sheriff Gary Hughes was John Hughes's brother. Although Sheriff Hughes had properly turned the case over to Captain Doug Emmons to avoid any appearance of vendetta, it still went without saying that this was one man that the Johnson County Sheriff's Department very badly wanted to bring in. "I'd been on the radio in a serious manner because we were getting spread pretty thin," Henderson said. There were no other law-enforcement officers in the immediate area. As he began to reach the end of his police radio range, Henderson decided he would have to pull Burr over all by himself, so he hit the light and siren switches, turning "all of it on."

Dale did not speed up when Henderson started signaling him to pull over, but he did not slow down immediately either. He drove on for at least a half-mile before finally slowing and turning left onto another section line road, where he continued north perhaps one hundred feet and parked the truck on the side of the road between two cornfields.

Henderson stopped at the intersection about thirty yards behind Dale's truck and continued to call for reinforcements by radio. He could see Dale moving around in the cab with his gun, but he held his fire.

11

Although Deputy Henderson did not know it, Dale had a purpose in stopping where he did. From where he sat in the cab of his truck, he could see almost the entire Siever place.

On the horizon to the north in a group of bare trees sat the old Siever home, a severe, two-story farmhouse that was noteworthy for one feature: In a region where white houses are the general rule, it was the only red house for miles around.

The Siever barn no longer stood, but Dale had put in four large metal bins for storing corn where the old barn used to be. Farther behind the house there were a couple of metal-roofed sheds and a ruined old windmill with its rudder hanging at a forlorn angle.

The real attraction of the Siever place in Dale's eyes, though, was the land, which sloped down from the red house on the horizon in a 160-acre swath with a swale in the middle. Dale had done his erosion-control work with the Soil Conservation Service here, building a series of earthen check dams across the low land to catch eroding top-soil and stabilize the field.

It was a project that one neighbor said nine out of ten farmers would not have undertaken, but one that mattered a great deal to Dale. He spent $20,000 out of his own pocket, and in the end he was successful in reducing soil erosion on Section 35. One of the most obvious signs of Dale's effort was at the intersection where Deputy Henderson was at that moment parked. Before Dale built his check dams, the lower part of his property used to wash across the road at the intersection every year.

Perhaps Dale Burr was amused by the private knowledge that he had helped make the law officer's parking place safe; perhaps he was engaged in other thoughts. Years of his dreams and labor had been wrapped up in this piece of land. It was the one that was really his—the first one that he had bought himself. He paid cash for the entire 160 acres, and then a few years later he bought the eighty next to it from Bill Hotz in West Liberty, and paid cash for that too. Dale's hand was evident in almost everything, from the tidiness of his newly harvested fields to the good-looking hog-wire fence running alongside the road.

When Henderson began talking through his bullhorn, Dale reached for his model 31. Glancing in his mirror, Dale could see that the deputy had gotten out and taken up a position behind the patrol car. Dale opened the box of ammunition on the seat beside him and reloaded the shot-gun. He glanced at the deputy, who appeared to be talking on the radio again. This gave Dale the little bit more time he needed. He took a deep breath and watched its steam turn to frost in the open window of the truck.

Without turning the engine off, he flipped the gun over so that the butt was against the floor and the barrel was pointing toward him. It is not the easiest thing to aim a shotgun at yourself in the narrow confines of a pickup cab, but Dale managed the trick by skewing the gun off to the passenger's side. Then he nestled the warm muzzle of the shotgun against the center of his chest, as close as he could to his heart. One last look, one last thought, and he pulled the trigger.

Dale was undoubtedly amazed and enraged when he did not die. How could his model 31 fail him now? Then, between agonized gasps, he realized what had happened. He had shot himself point-blank in the chest, but because of the way he had the gun angled, the shot only shattered ribs and a portion of his left arm without passing through any vital organs. He was now in tremendous pain, but very much alive. With his right hand he fought the Remington's pump lever back to eject the spent shell and bring a fresh shell into the chamber.

Dale Burr's last labor may very well have been his hardest. He had a three-centimeter-wide hole in his side, which rendered his left arm useless. A great deal of shotgun shell wadding and powder burned into the margin of the wound, and he was bleeding heavily. Finally, he managed to pump the gun one-handed. Now he swung around in the pool of blood on the seat and repositioned the gun on the floor, determined that there be no mistakes. He may have cried out in pain and sorrow then, but no one heard his voice any more than they heard the sound of the shots he fired.

A moment or two later, Henderson was joined by reinforcements. One of the first was Johnson County Sheriff's Captain Duane Lewis, who noted no movement in Burr's truck when he arrived at 11:55 A.M. Captain Lewis talked to Dale through the bullhorn while the cars of other officers lined up behind Henderson's. By 11:58, there were at least six officers on hand, but they were still reluctant to flush Dale. The thing that changed their minds was the arrival of off-duty Iowa State Patrol Sergeant Dan Jahnke. An acquaintance of Dale and Emily's who had heard about the shootings on the radio, Jahnke came in from the north, parking fifty yards on the other side of Dale's truck. Then he got out and began walking toward Dale's truck, alone and apparently unarmed.

Seeing that Jahnke intended to take Dale right then, the group of officers back at the intersection sprung into action. "We were in kind of an awkward position," recalled David Henderson, "because Jahnke was in our line of fire if we had to cover him." Captain Lewis and Iowa State Patrol Officer William Kean started toward Dale's truck with their guns drawn. They could see Dale sitting in the window of the truck. He was slumped to one side as if he was asleep or playing possum. Lewis arrived at the truck first. He cautiously opened the door on the driver's side while Kean opened the door on the passenger's side and drew a bead on Dale. As Jahnke neared the truck, Lewis checked Dale's wrist for a pulse, and then reached in and turned the truck off.

Dale was dead, sitting upright in his truck with his Sweet Lassy hat still on his head. His last shot had done its work well, catching him full in the chest and blowing a hole through his heart and lungs, much as he had done to Emily. The gun ended up cradled in his arms beside the nine unfired shells remaining from the box he'd bought from Dennis Busch that morning. The biting cold made the law officers turn their backs to the north wind, but Dale sat unmoved. His part was over. It was one minute before noon, and not quite an hour had elapsed since he began his rampage.

Officer Kean removed Dale's Remington model 31 from the cab of the truck, but otherwise they left him sitting as they found him as a crowd of law officers, news reporters, and curious locals gathered around the remote intersection. After conferring briefly, Lewis and Jahnke decided to go together to notify Emily at the nearby Burr house. They pulled into the driveway at 12:08. With Jahnke leading the way, the two officers went around to the back door and knocked. There was no answer, so they peered through the window. At first, they saw nothing, but then, when their eyes fell to the floor, they were horrified. There was Emily in a pool of blood.

She was lying on her back staring at the ceiling, like a domino that had been knocked over. A bandanna still covered her hair curlers, and the cookie batter still sat out on the counter. Blood and flesh were splattered against the far wall. Checking the rest of the house, the officers found hunks of shotgun wadding that had been blown through Emily and ended up twenty or more feet away in the living room. From the gaping, star-shaped hole where her heart used to be, Jahnke and Lewis concluded that Emily must have been another of Dale's victims. Suddenly, they wondered how many more people he might have left lying in their own blood that morning.

By 12:11 P.M., when Jahnke called from the Burr house and reported Emily's death, law-enforcement officers were pouring into Hills from all over. One of the first to arrive on the scene at the Hills Bank was Rick SyWassink of the Iowa Division of Criminal Investigation. Even before Officers Lewis, Kean, and Jahnke found Dale dead in his truck, SyWassink was on the phone to headquarters in Des Moines, where he spoke briefly with Thomas Ruxton, director of the Iowa Division of Criminal Investigation. Put in charge of the investigation and promised all the support he needed, SyWassink "assumed a command post in the vacant office of the Hills Bank and Trust Company and at that time began assigning leads and organizing the investigation."

Around him at the Hills Bank, the horror was beginning to drive home. "There was a lot of sobbing and crying that day," said Roy Justice, marketing officer for the bank, "and not just among the women." With the doors of the bank locked to outsiders, except the steadily increasing number of law-enforcement officers, the bank's employees tried to piece together what had happened and why. Slowly, employees who had fled returned. Among the last were Angie Feldman and Krista Kirkpatrick (Dale's cousin, with whom he had spoken before going in to see Roger Reilly). When the shooting started, Feldman and Kirkpatrick had run outside and hidden in a maintenance shed beside the bank. Later, they moved to Stutsman's store, where they remained until 12:15.

Fearing now that John Burr might also be a victim, law officers on the scene redoubled their efforts to find the next of kin. No one knew where John Burr was, because the last two people who spoke to him—and the people most likely to know—were both dead. For nearly three-quarters of an hour the tension grew, until finally they discovered him only a couple hundred yards away at his grandmother's farm on the other side of the Parizek place. He had been tending his hogs and had no idea what had been going on. The police rushed John back to his parents' house. Before he went inside, though, the police decided he should go somewhere else to call his sisters and inform them of the news. Jahnke reentered the house and got John a clean change of clothes from his upstairs bedroom. With these in hand, John went to the nearby home of his uncle, Lloyd Burr, Jr., where he called his sisters, Sheila and Julia.

When Bob Berry heard that his cousin and hunting partner had killed at least one person, he called the pastor of Our Redeemer Lutheran Church. As quickly as possible, Berry, his wife, Glorine, and Rev. Robert Bailey rushed to the Burr home. When they arrived a little after one P.M. they expected to comfort Emily, but a law officer intercepted them before they got to the door. "Emily's gone," he said. Soon they were joined by other relatives, among them Al Burr, who had been one of the first members of the Prairie Masters 4-H chapter. More and more law officers and forensic specialists arrived during the afternoon, as did press photographers from Iowa City, Des Moines, Chicago, and New York.

Around four P.M., Tom and Cindy Haggard, who rented the Parizek home from John Burr, came over to feed the animals. John himself returned home about fifteen minutes after that and began tending to the evening chores around the curtilage. At five P.M., Thomas Ruxton and Johnson County Prosecuting Attorney Pat White arrived at the Burr place. They toured the scene of Emily's murder and consulted with officers on hand. A short time later, they were joined by Emily's brother-in-law, Calvin Schmidt of Tipton, and John Burr's girl friend, Jan See.

By night, an air of normalcy had returned to the Burr farm. The big old white house was quiet, and a few lights burned in the windows. Three wagons full of grain sat in the farmyard, and neighbors tended hogs back by the barn. Except for the police car parked in the drive and the two officers standing guard, it might have been any other December evening after dinner.

★　　★　　★

In the other houses that were scattered across the winter landscape of Johnson County that night, however, affairs were far from normal. Ordinarily tight-lipped and disinclined to dwell openly on the problems of others, the people of Johnson County suddenly could talk of nothing else.

One of the hardest hit was Harold Schuessler, Dale's next-door neighbor and a director of the Hills Bank. "It was nippy and Doris was just leaving to take her mother a cake for her ninety-first birthday at the rest home," Schuessler recalled of December 9. "I was sitting here at the kitchen table eating lunch and listening to the radio when the news bulletin came on the Cedar Rapids station saying there'd been a tragedy at the Hills Bank.

"I got up and ran outside to the garage—went right out into the snow in my stocking feet—and told her about it." Doris Schuessler was one of Emily's best friends, one of the "robin bunch." "She asked if I wanted her to take the truck so I'd have the car if I had to go into the bank. I said 'No, I can drive the truck,' and I went back inside to listen to the radio. Then the phone rang. It was Tim [Smith] from the bank. I said I just heard that John Hughes had been shot and asked who did it. He said, 'Your next-door neighbor.' Man, I mean to tell you it was like you hit me over the head with a two-by-four."

Another neighbor, Floyd Hotz, looked out his front window toward the Burr farmstead a mile to the north. "You sit here and look over there and think it's a dream," he said. "A nightmare," added his wife, Betty, who was another close friend of Emily's. A neighbor to the west, James Buline, commented on the developments of the previous day, "If it's affecting everybody in this community like it's affecting me, everybody in this town is pretty shook up." Buline called the shootings a "terrible tragedy" that defied logic. "We're all just sitting here this afternoon trying to get it through our heads. Gosh, I had his kids in 4-H."

Some, like Dale's old friend and cousin Leland Stock, were aware of the deeper implications of the shootings. "We're losing farmers," he said. "We're losing the survivors. . . . And I'll tell you: Them guys is tough old birds. They've seen it all. . . . If farming would have been paying off, Dale would have farmed *forever,* wouldn't he?" Stock asked, nodding at his wife, Adeline. "He'd never have shot that beautiful wife or that friendly banker or that young farmer with two kids." Stock began to sob softly. "It just looked awful big. You couple that with pride and maybe some weakness in your personality. And that's the soup you get. Some people can handle debt, and some people can't. And he was born without debt."

The reaction of the wider community was no less stunned. "Nobody thought Dale would do anything like that," said an acquaintance. "He was quiet, didn't smoke or drink, didn't socialize much. His life was his wife and that farm of his." In the Hills Tap, a tavern at the other end of the block from the Hills Bank, the conversation on the evening of December 9 was relentlessly one-track. "It's a sad situation for the whole country," said one Hills area farmer who, unlike Dale, had already finished his major fall work and therefore was able to take the day off. "I was skinnin' a deer when I heard it over the radio, and my hand got to shakin' so hard I had to quit if I didn't want to cut myself." His wife reported a similar reaction: "I'd just gone Christmas shopping, but when I heard about this on the radio, I just couldn't shop anymore."

Pat White, Johnson County Attorney, recalls how "there was an extraordinary level of fear afterward. The nature of John Hughes's death really horrified people. There was a lot more door locking, and people were literally whispering to me about the subject in the Hy-Vee [supermarket] where I shop." Within an hour of the shootings, an unidentified man called Marty Robinson, Ag banker at the Iowa State Bank in Iowa City, and said, "You're next." Dan Levitas of Prairiefire, a Des Moines group active in rural crisis counseling, said, "For many of these people, the hammer is coming down. They're shell-shocked. Many keep it all inside. But now it's breaking out. I'm afraid this violence is the beginning of what is to come."

Tom Huston, state banking superintendent and head of the Columbus Junction Bank, said, "I told the governor [of Iowa] two and a half years ago that we would see some sort of uprising brought on by the farm economy. A farmer becomes unhappy with a person who tells him he is not doing well financially. Oftentimes, the first person to tell the farmer that he is in financial trouble is his lender." Huston's comments were particularly telling, since his bank had turnèd Dale Burr down when he had come in begging for money two days before the shooting. John Crystal, president of Bankers Trust in Des Moines and a friend of Hughes, said, "I'm sorry for everybody. I don't think terrible things are bound to happen, but shootings like this might happen again."

Others were outraged at the suggestion that Dale's actions were somehow inevitable or justified by his circumstances. "We are too readily saying now that this could happen to anyone," said Pat White, who had been in law school with John Hughes. "I hear too many people saying we're surprised it hasn't happened before. I'm concerned about this attitude because this was a brutal, cold-blooded murder. No one has any excuse for doing what he did." James Gannon, the influential editor of the *Des Moines*

Register, wrote, "Dale Burr did not 'go out in a blaze of glory,' as one neighbor remarked—it was a blaze of shame. This was not a case of a hard-nosed banker pushing a hard-luck farmer to the wall. Unlike hundreds of other Iowa farmers, Burr was not being foreclosed upon. He had debt troubles, but the Hills Bank was planning to finance him again in 1986."

If Dale were alive, he undoubtedly would have been interested to hear that the Hills Bank had planned to continue financing him. What he knew was that the bank had been threatening in writing to foreclose on the Burr home place since May. Within the last few months, the bank had been declaring its intent by calling every loan with him as it came due. Neither Dale nor Emily was alive to tell their side of the story, however, so the Hills Bank and Trust's account of its financial relationship with the Burrs went unchallenged. James Gordon, Hills Bank and Trust vice-president, said, "We were working with him on his finances. I think he had some problems he was concerned about and we were concerned about. The bank wasn't going to foreclose on him, though."

There is no telling what repercussions the Lone Tree tragedy might have provoked if the real story had been known, but even so, Dale Burr's dark hour had undeniable impact. The story of the terrible thing that happened that morning in the small towns of Hills and Lone Tree, Iowa, went on to make news all over the world. In fact, one friend of John Hughes read about it in Djakarta. It seemed that people everywhere found it newsworthy that a Midwestern American farmer who seemingly had so many advantages over the millions of poor farmers who populate most of the rest of the world would feel compelled by financial distress to kill himself and those around him.

The morning after the killings, December 10, 1985, Representative Kika de la Garza, chairman of the U.S. House of Representatives' Agriculture Committee, invoked Dale's name in a last-ditch drive to win passage of a financial bailout of the foundering Farm Credit System. "Time is running out," de la Garza told the full House. "Time ran out for Dale Burr yesterday." De la Garza, a south Texas Democrat, went on to say that "perhaps if we had sent down this [bill] last week, Dale Burr would be alive today. . . . If he'd had word that Congress cared . . . that somebody cared . . . maybe Dale Burr would be alive today." De la Garza called on Congress to "send a message" to farmers "on the brink" that it was not blind to their plight.

The bill that was approved that day by a vote of 393 to 32 was part of the complex package that comprised the Farm Act of 1985. Passed after eleven months of emotional debate, the Farm Act was designed to cut federal support to agriculture, provide additional backing for the Farm Credit System, and promote conservation through the removal of marginal land from production. President Ronald Reagan's advisers believed that cutting farm support would reduce both the federal deficit and interest rates, thereby cutting costs for farm borrowers. It was believed that this in turn would spur the sale of American farm produce overseas by reducing the cost of production, and ultimately the prices that American farmers could charge and still make a profit.

Many farmers, however, saw the effects of the Farm Act in much less convoluted and flattering terms. As during the days of the Nixon Administration, the principal mechanism that the Reagan Administration intended to use to reduce U.S. agricultural prices was cutting federal support for

American farmers. This meant less government investment in all facets of the nation's largest industry, and most important, less money guaranteed by the government for their crops. With thousands of farmers like Dale already pressed to the wall—or beyond—such a policy seemed to promote not stable farm production, but rather more foreclosures and the tragic unraveling of the traditional core of American society.

Chuck Frazier, a Washington, D.C., representative of the National Farm Organization, said, "A lot of farmers are going broke at the present rates. What's going to happen when they lower them?" Most observers agreed that the Farm Act of 1985 would favor large farmers over small ones, and accelerate the exodus of farmers from the land. "If you believe we need to have a program that will produce food the cheapest way possible and be competitive abroad, then this is a good bill," said independent farm economist Edwin Jaenke. "But if you feel that we need to help desperate farmers get back on their feet, then this is a very poor bill."

As enacted, the Farm Act of 1985 represented a mixed bag of often conflicting impulses, strategies, and beliefs produced by a Democratic Congress under threat of veto by a Republican President. The fundamental thrust was President Reagan's, however, and marked the second time in two decades that a Republican President had set in motion policies designed to accelerate the American enclosures.

Despite the fact that he spent his early years broadcasting football games for WHO Radio in Davenport, Iowa, Reagan the President was not notably sympathetic to the problems of Iowa farmers. In 1985 he joked at the Gridiron Club, "I think we should keep the grain and export the farmers."

When Reagan signed the bill on Christmas Eve 1985, he complained of the cost of the measure, but declared that the Farm Act "provides new hope for America's hard-working farmers and our rural communities."

12

John Hughes was buried on Wednesday, December 11, two days after the shootings. As the media was excluded from the private burial at Memory Gardens Cemetery in Iowa City, enterprising photographers stationed themselves in a nearby trailer court.

The photos they got through their telephoto lenses show the Hughes family striding together through the snow. Karen Hughes, John's widow, has a daughter on each arm while Gary Hughes, John's brother, follows behind. All are looking down, and Karen's eyes are darkened. She has obviously been crying, but she looks strong and resilient too.

An estimated fifteen hundred people—including most of the prominent citizens of Johnson County—gathered an hour later for Hughes's memorial service at St. Andrew's Presbyterian Church. There were so many people that they overflowed into the flower-lined halls of the capacious downtown church. People were still squeezing through the front door when the service began.

In keeping with the ecumenical spirit of the man being memorialized, ministers of several faiths spoke. One of the most eloquent was Rev. Henry Greiner of St. Mary's Catholic Church in Iowa City. Father Greiner prayed:

> We who live in rural America are in trouble, Lord— not because we have not worked long and hard. As a matter of fact, Lord, the harder we work, the more desperate the situation becomes. Lord, all we ask is that our President and elected officials will not be deaf to the cry of those who till the soil and feed the nation. . . . Lord, we ask that the sound of these shots, so desperate and so insane, will rouse the conscience of this nation so that we might realize there is more lasting peace and security in a bushel of beans than there is in a whole bunker of bullets.

Rev. Alvin Desterhaft, pastor of St. Andrew, made the closing comments. He had known John Hughes personally, and his church had benefited from the banker's presence in the congregation. Emotionally, the tragedy seemed to have hit him like a punch. "I cannot prophesy the good that will come of this," he told one of the largest throngs ever to attend his church. "Only God knows how to turn that which is bizarre, senseless, and evil, and bring something that is good." The mourners rose and sang "Joy to the World."

Afterward, friends, associates, and even casual acquaintances remembered John Hughes as a good person. "If ever there was a guy who was sympathetic to farmers, it was John Hughes," said Tam Ormiston, an assistant Iowa attorney general who had known the banker. "He was striking in his genuine interest in helping them. He was working not only in his own bank, but also with other banks. The

Hills Bank and Trust also had an extraordinarily good reputation for working with its farmer customers." Hills Bank vice-president James Gordon echoed this view. "He knew what farmers were going through," said Gordon. "That stress took a toll on John."

By comparison, Rich Goody was the forgotten man of the tragedy, largely because of the attitude of the Goody family. Apart from Marvin Goody—who described his cousin as "easygoing and a hard worker"—no one else said anything at all, despite considerable pressure. On Monday evening, the Goodys were approached by the *Des Moines Register* for a photo of Rich, but the family refused to cooperate, even though the *Register* reporter convinced the family priest to intervene on the paper's behalf. As a result, the next day's *Des Moines Register* featured a line of photographs showing the victims of the tragedy: Dale Burr, Emily Burr, John Hughes—and Rich Goody's mailbox.

Rich Goody was buried the day after John Hughes. Overnight the clouds had cleared, and Thursday, December 12, dawned clear and even colder. The temperature barely rose above zero all day, despite the unsparing glare of the winter sun. At noon more than 250 people attended the traditional closed-casket service for Rich Goody at St. Joseph's Catholic Church in Hills, overflowing the small-town facility. Where Rich Goody had worshiped quietly with his family and a few others at the midnight service four days before, now there were hundreds of people, among them Johnson County Sheriff Gary Hughes.

Marilyn, Rachel, and Mark Goody trailed behind the casket to the front of the church. The children looked terrified and clung to their mother, who sobbed quietly. It looked as though Marilyn would regain control, and then her shoulders started to heave again like a small boat on a sea of despair. Although it had received considerable floral attention that day, St. Joseph's remained an irredeemably plain building. Inside, where a welter of saints and icons march around the green walls, the church boasted one touch of beauty: a stained-glass window that contained a lovingly rendered scene of rolling green fields that could have been Iowa. The low winter sun charged the windows with light as Rev. David Hitch of St. Joseph's stepped forward to deliver his memorial sermon for Rich Goody.

Father Hitch was not particularly close to the young farmer, but he liked him and got a strong sense of his virtues through Marilyn, who was increasingly active in the church. A stocky man with an air of intellectuality, Father Hitch spoke well, with a rich voice and a sense of drama that held the audience, even though many of them could not actually see him. In his sermon, he contrasted the events of Sunday, December 8, to those of the next day. On Sunday, Rich had taken his elderly mother, Wilma, and six-year-old son, Mark, with him to cut down the family Christmas tree, which they brought back to the house that evening. "And then the events of Monday," Hitch said. "How can we ever comprehend the absolute horror Marilyn must have experienced that morning?"

Like Father Greiner, he saw the tragedy that had visited Johnson County, Iowa, that week as symptomatic of a larger malaise. "American agriculture, small rural towns, and their way of life are in crisis," he said. "Policy decisions made on the highest levels of our government seem bent on eliminating the small family farm. In the early 1960s, there were seven million farms in our country. Today, there are two and a half million." All four of the dead, including Dale Burr, were "victims of this policy," according to Father Hitch. "Don't get me wrong. Dale Burr did a stupid thing, a terrible thing. He is responsible for what he did and may God have mercy on his soul. And yet, he too was caught up in this vortex called farm debt."

In conclusion, Rev. Hitch directed the mourners' attention to the Bible. "My hope today as we gather to support and comfort this family is that we all heed long and hard the dream of Isaiah—that we melt down our weapons of destruction into plowshares and sickles and other means of livelihood." An American flag was draped over Rich Goody's casket, and the American Legion read a poem traditionally used to honor war veterans. There was no rifle salute when the casket was taken from the church, however, at Marilyn Goody's direction. When asked if she wanted the full military service to which her husband was entitled because of his Vietnam service, Marilyn said, "No! No more guns."

Dale and Emily Burr were buried the next day, Friday the thirteenth of December 1985. Before the funeral, John Burr invited old friends to come by to pay their respects and view Dale and Emily's remains if they desired. One person who went said afterward she wished she had not. Despite the considerable efforts of the mortician ("autopsy and special restoration" was the single largest item on the Burrs' bill from Sordens Funeral Home), the sight was not a pretty one. The twin caskets were closed for the traditional ceremony at Our Redeemer Lutheran Church, as were the doors of the Missouri Synod church to nonmembers of the congregation. One member of the parish reported that Rev. Robert Bailey "preached a sermon to the living," adding that he "didn't condemn anyone."

Less than half the two hundred mourners who attended the Iowa City church service made the ten-mile journey to the cemetery in Lone Tree where the Burrs were laid to rest. Normally, this would have been an impressive funeral procession, but it was the smallest of the funerals for the victims of the Lone Tree tragedy. On the way into the Lone Tree Cemetery, the long line of cars streamed by the grave of Rich Goody with its cross and fresh flowers. That day the two black hearses' destination was a little higher up the rise, to the Burr family plot immediately behind the large impressive-looking headstone of Dale's father, Vernon Burr. This was as close to a hill as anything around, and from it you could see most of Lone Tree, the American Legion hall where Dale had made the speech about what farming meant to him, the site of the old "Burr Bank," the World War II–vintage tank in the town park, and a flock of sheep chewing their cud in the field beyond.

Dale and Emily's identical wooden coffins, each adorned with bouquets of red roses and white carnations, were set on wheeled dollies before the single large grave that would soon receive them, side by side. The Burr family arrayed themselves on folding chairs under an awning, with John Burr seated in the center, between the two coffins. Photographs show him staring straight ahead with a squinty-eyed, faraway gaze. His sisters, Sheila and Julia, were there with him, as were Dale's sister, Ruth Forbes, and her husband, Keith, and other members of the immediate family. Behind them stood fifty friends and relatives. Rev. Bailey read quickly through the graveside burial service in the three-degree-below-zero cold, and then they put Dale and Emily in the ground.

Afterward, the community quickly moved to support all the victims. Thursday, December 12, the day of the Goody funeral, a group of Lone Tree neighbors got together to harvest the portion of Dale's crop that still remained in the fields. Fifteen people and three combines were involved, and by dark they had gotten it all, filling the Burr farmyard with wagons heaped with corn and beans. Another friend paid for fuel oil, and yet others made sure that Dale's surviving horses got fed and watered. In January, nineteen hundred people turned out for a benefit pork sausage breakfast for Marilyn Goody at the Hills Community Center. Flanked by Wilma Goody and Father Hitch, Marilyn Goody told reporters she would use the money raised by the breakfast for her children.

There was obviously a great deal of concern over what had happened, but people were also becoming weary of the affair, too. "I have put four white crosses up in front of the church as a memorial, and nobody has asked me why they are there," complained Father Hitch. "We held a prayer vigil the week before Christmas and only forty-six people showed up." It was apparent that the people of Johnson County did not want to be in the vanguard of the farm struggle, or channel their sorrow into a political outlet. They just wanted the whole thing to go away. The more they thought about it, the worse it made them feel about all sorts of things.

Partly as a defense against further hurt, community attitudes toward the tragedy hardened. This is not to say that there was agreement about the incident, however, for a sizable gap separated the neighboring towns of Hills and Lone Tree. In Hills, where the death of John Hughes hit particularly hard, people tended to see Dale Burr as a person who was bound to fail. "He was a fuckup, from start to finish," said one person. "He had land, a good start, a beautiful wife, and what did he do but fritter it away? He even fucked up at the end. He couldn't even kill himself with the first shot. When you think of it, that was perfect Dale Burr. It took two shots to commit suicide!"

In Lone Tree, feelings were somewhat different. Here

people were more aware of Dale's virtues and the faults of the others. They did not see this excusing what Dale did, but it made them susceptible to a more complex melancholy that was probably expressed best in the sayings of the oracle of Lone Tree, Mrs. Grynneth Parizek. For the past decade, the widowed "Mrs. P.," as she is known around town, had published aphorisms and admonitions that seem to come from sources as diverse as Chinese fortune cookies and the Bible.

Her medium is hand-lettered signs nailed to the telephone pole in front of Lone Tree High School. Over the years, she had slowly pulverized the thick wooden pole with her nails, like some oversized cat sharpening its claws. Her spot is well chosen for the community, though. Almost everyone goes through the intersection in front of school at some time during the day, and with the signs posted at eye level of a person in a car, they get tremendous local readership.

Mostly she favors a general miscellany, but after the shootings her thoughts seemed to be running on a subject of deep interest to the people of Lone Tree. "You can't keep a chip on your shoulder when you're carrying your own weight," said one. Another observed, "Some people do odd things to get even."

Less than a month after Dale Burr's rampage, fears of a new wave of farm evictions spread across America when the FmHA announced it was ending a two-year moratorium on foreclosures. The federal agency said it would be sending "pay up" notices to seventy thousand farmers, one-quarter of its farm borrowers.

The FmHA had tried to begin foreclosuring on delinquent farmers earlier during the Reagan Administration, but had been prevented by court order. Then, on March 5,

1986, a federal judge ruled that the FmHA could proceed with its evictions, as long as the people who were being fore-closed were informed of their "rights." Anticipating too much work for it to handle, the FmHA decided to hire private collection agencies to shake the past-due loans out of farmers.

Texas Agriculture Commissioner Jim Hightower said the FmHA action amounted to declaring war on its own bor-rowers. "What the FmHA is doing, Jesse James got shot for," said Hightower. An FmHA spokesman responded that there were "a lot of people out there who are farming who shouldn't be farming." Said FmHA Administrator Vance Clark, "We're going to lose a lot of farmers this year, and we've got to accept that."

Aggravating the situation in Iowa and elsewhere in the Midwest were bumper harvests of many crops. The 1985 corn crop was 8.9 billion bushels, the largest in U.S. his-tory. A record five billion bushels of American corn were still in storage in July of the next year, along with a record 1.9 billion bushels of wheat. This meant slack demand and a 35 percent commodity price decline at a time when the government was actually paying more, since it was obliged to purchase and store a great deal of corn that could not be sold at home or abroad.

These developments provoked strident attacks on the Farm Act. *Barron's* and other members of the conservative financial press found such public expenses for agriculture outrageous, even though direct federal support of farmers had dropped from 4.6 percent of the government's budget in 1950 to .9 percent in 1984. At the same time, Midwestern farmers found the bill a prescription for their destruction. They were particularly upset that while small family farm-ers were being cut out, large operators were receiving huge sums of money from the government in direct subsidies.

Among the large farmers receiving substantial government subsidies were J. G. Boswell, a California company that is one of the nation's major cotton producers. In 1986, Boswell qualified for $20 million in government subsidies. Another California operation, owned by U.S. citizen Mohamed Aslam Khan and four Pakistani passive investors, got $152,000 for their rice farm in Butte City, California. Nor were the recipients of federal farm subsidies all full-time farmers. For instance, Frederick Joseph, chief executive of Drexel Burnham Lambert Inc., received subsidies for his 160-acre hobby dairy farm in upstate New York. Under the Farm Act of 1985, large farmers got even more, as Secretary of Agriculture John Block acknowledged.

Perhaps the bitterest twist of all was the effect that the Farm Credit bailout had on farm lending. Although Representative de la Garza presented the bailout as a way of aiding failing farmers like Dale Burr, it did not work that way. As a FmHA report concluded in 1986, "The existence of the financial assistance package will not appreciably improve the system's ability to forebear in 1986." In Iowa, state-chartered banks had more deposits relative to loans in March 1986 than they had in September 1985, indicating an increasing unwillingness of bankers to loan money to farmers. The most significant result of the bailout appeared to be the system's direct line to the federal Treasury. As Iowa Senator Tom Harkin observed, the bill bailed out the farm bankers but not the farm borrowers.

Nor did the export bonanza foreseen by the Reagan Administration materialize. In 1986, U.S. farm exports dipped to $27 billion, down 12 percent from the year before, and 37 percent since the 1981 high-water mark. In May 1986, the U.S. actually became a net importer of farm products for the first extended period since 1959. "Something is radically wrong when the greatest food producer in the world is buying more agricultural commodities than it is selling," said Kansas Senator Robert Dole. "This trend simply cannot continue." It did continue, though, as the U.S. ran a record trade deficit of $34.7 billion in the second quarter of 1986. This period also saw the U.S. become the largest debtor nation in the world, outstripping number-two Brazil by more than $50 billion.

Meanwhile, the U.S. Office of Technology Assessment predicted that half of America's 2.2 million farms would be eliminated over the next fourteen years. Such a decline would economically devastate many small American farm communities. One-third of Iowa's implement dealers had already gone out of business over the previous six years, and with them went basic services like gas stations, grocery stores, and schools. In the face of this, former Secretary of Agriculture Butz lambasted the news media for playing up only the bad news and ignoring "the nearly one-half of the farmers" who are not in debt. Butz, seventy-six, derided efforts to save the family farm as the work of "bleeding hearts."

Down on the farm, though, the bleeding hearts were real. On January 8, 1986, less than a month after Dale Burr's rampage, Bruce Litchfield, an FmHA county supervisor, killed his wife, thirteen-year-old daughter, and nine-year-old son while they slept in their Elk Point, South Dakota, home. Litchfield, thirty-eight, was apparently upset because he had just learned that new FmHA regulations would force him to foreclose on many borrowers. Then, on February 4, less than a month after the Elk Point tragedy, a Waynesboro, Georgia, farmer killed himself a half hour before his farm was to be auctioned off on the county courthouse steps. L. D. Hill, sixty-seven, told his wife how much life insurance he had and how it might be used to save the family's farm. Then he went in the bedroom and shot himself.

The South was perhaps the hardest hit. A survey by the American Banking Association in 1985 showed that more Southern farmers had reached their credit limit or gone out of business than in any other area of the country. Georgia Agriculture Commissioner Tommy Irvin predicted, "We may lose up to ten percent of the state's index of fifty thousand farmers and ranchers, and of that fifty thousand, probably twenty-five thousand are in trouble." The spreading crisis engulfed even the best farmers, including the notoriously thrifty Georgia Mennonites. Among those forced out was retired baseball star Gaylord Perry, who filed for bankruptcy in August 1986 on his four-hundred-acre North Carolina farm. "I can't see anybody making it in farming these days," said Perry, who raised corn, tobacco, and peanuts. "It's like selling ice in Alaska. There's no future in it."

Even some farmers in the most favorable Western situations found themselves in trouble. By the summer of 1986, land prices for rich (and heavily subsidized) irrigated land in Washington's Columbia Basin had begun to plummet for the first time since the Depression. When land values fell, bankers began calling portions of loans that had been extended with the land as collateral. Then, when farmers tried to unload their expensive machinery to pay off the loans, they found that the value of machinery had dropped in half. The State of Washington, which counts agriculture as its largest industry, estimated that 10 percent of its thirty-eight thousand farmers would be out of business by the end of the year.

And so the process continues. Looking back over half a millennium at the farmers who had been sacrificed to enclosure, one gets the impression that our culture harvests its farmers, just as the farmer harvests his crops. Generation after generation they have been sown, nurtured for the strength they provide in their prime, and then sent down before the scythe of industrial society. It is hard to see history happen. Its processes, like the opening of a flower, are generally too slow to observe, but the speed of the American farmers' dispossession has almost been fast enough to follow with the naked eye. During this century, the breakup of agrarian America has become the largest forced migration in the history of the world: forty million people in fifty years.

For the great majority of its history, America has been an agricultural nation. Most of its people have earned their living from farming, and farming has been the most valuable national product. Traditionally, the visible growth of the country has been measured in extension of cultivated lands. "This progressive taking-over and settlement of the farming lands is the most impressive material achievement of the American people," wrote Thorstein Veblen, "as it is also the most serviceable work which they have accomplished hitherto." Farmers were the ones who "won" the West, just as they have won and lost virtually every other struggle in the nation's history, for until the end of World War I, the words *American* and *farmer* were generally synonymous.

We can see the great foundation of agricultural experience that underlies modern American culture in the expressions that still occur commonly in American speech: make hay while the sun shines, high on the hog, mad as a wet hen, corny, sheepish, turkey—and that pointed euphemism for death—to buy the farm. Politically, farmers have had an equally deep effect on the nature of America, especially its long, tumultuous relationship with democracy. Thomas Jefferson thought the small farmer was the surest safeguard of democratic liberty. "Those who labor in the earth are the chosen people of God," he wrote. "Generally speaking, the proportion which the aggregate of the other classes of citizens bears in any state to that of its husbandmen, is the proportion of its unsound to its healthy parts, and is a good enough barometer whereby to measure its degree of corruption."

The freedom of the frontier bred an independent people who were as different from their European brethren as the laws that governed them. While eighteenth-century English poor laws required people to give up their family cow and other means of subsistence and self-respect to get on the dole, the American government under Thomas Jefferson was making good land available as fast as free yeomen could be found to claim it. The land drew people from all over the world, but it was more than simple greed that made America a mecca for immigrants. Freedom to feed yourself—and with that the freedom to think and speak as you chose—was paramount. "Well, so I come West, just like a thousand other fellers, to get a start where the cussed European aristocracy hadn't got a holt on the people," commented an immigrant farmer in Hamlin Garland's *Main Travelled Roads*. "I'm my own boss," he added, "and I'm going to stay my own boss if I have to live on crackers an' wheat coffee to do it; that's the kind of hair-pin I am."

It was people like this who gave America its reputation for inventiveness and physical toughness. While town men live by their specialties, the farmer has traditionally lived by mastering many interrelated skills. He could build a barn, milk a cow, butcher a hog, ditch a field, and fix almost anything with baling wire. He was acquainted with the realms of finance and foreign trade, could make his opinions heard passably in public meetings, and serve as an effective soldier or statesman when the need arose. According to Wendell Berry, "The good farmer (like the artist, the quarterback, the statesman) must be the master of many possible solutions, one of which he must choose under pressure and apply with skill in the right place at the right time."

In colonial times, the farmer was the sole craftsman of agriculture, assembling all the required elements in his own person. He grew his own seed, and like as not made his own plow, as was commonly done with the wooden plow of the period. Gradually at first, and then with increasing speed after the Civil War, American farmers embraced technological solutions to the problems they felt as a class. The cotton gin, the reaper, the combine, the milking machine, and countless other mechanical contrivances were adopted widely, even though the new technology generally penalized the free farmer in favor of the slave and the debtor. Technologically induced overproduction has been a constant problem in the United States since the end of World War I, but advancing farm technology has steadfastly remained the central tenet of American farm policy.

In our century, we have seen the introduction of the tractor and tremendous advances in the breeding and chemistry of farming which have utterly transformed the agricultural base of the country. Today, the farmer produces hardly anything involved in his farming activities, except perhaps the final beef or corn crop. The modern farmer is a juggler of farm ingredients, a consumer of technologies that are concocted and sold to him by large corporations. By the 1980s, more than two-thirds of the ingredients used in agriculture came from the "nonfarm sector" of the economy. Fewer and fewer farmers were small, because small farmers were unable to compete with the mechanized economies of scale, and fewer and fewer farmers were free of debt, since few could acquire the huge new machinery and land to match without going into debt.

Most surviving farmers—like the Burrs and Goodys—became specialists, concentrating on one type of livestock or field crop. Young farmers might remember how their grandfathers used to handle a scythe around fence posts or their fathers used to milk in the early dawn, but they had no more concrete idea of how to go about either of these tasks than someone who had seen it on TV. At the same time, complexity of farming increased tremendously. Far from being "simple," as they were often caricatured in the urban press, successful Midwestern farmers had to deal with economic intricacy undreamed of by most wage earners. Their livelihood was immediately affected by everything from the time they cut their hay to the size of the anchovita catch off Peru, which competes with soybean oil for some commercial uses. With government supports declining, it got harder every year for farmers all over the United States to make it.

"The farmhouse lights are going out all over America," said Oren Lee Stanley of the National Farm Organization. "And every time a light goes out, this country is losing something. It is losing the precious skills of a farm, a family system that has given this country unbounded wealth. And it is losing free men." Indeed, the greatest impact may well be the deep, delayed political one. A fundamental change has occurred in the social and economic underpinnings of our society. Like the environmental conditions that created the tall-grass prairie of the American Midwest thousands of years ago, the social conditions that produced America's democratic institutions are passing away. What does this mean for our future?

Once again, the American experience may be foretold in the history of England, and specifically the enclosures. J. L. and Barbara Hammond noted that for all the distress the enclosures caused, "the first consequence was not the worst consequence." Ultimately, the Hammonds believed the worst effect of the enclosures was that "the governing class by this policy killed the spirit of a race." Although other factors were involved, England's collapse to second-class-nation status followed soon after the country had finally destroyed its free yeomanry in the name of progress.

Similarly, the decline of Rome into corruption and impotence began with the destruction of the yeoman-farmer class that had been the backbone of the Roman army. All during the later Republic, the Roman countryside was convulsed by the process of enclosure, which saw large farms—or latifundia—appropriate the holdings of smaller Roman farmers. Latifundia were made possible by the cheap labor of slaves rather than machinery (as was the case in England and the United States after the Civil War), but the social consequences were much the same. In forcing small farmers off the land and driving them into the city to become part of the infamous Roman mob, the patrician class sowed the seeds of Rome's fall. Indeed, the death of the Republic came nearly as soon after the victory of the Roman enclosures as the fall of England came after the triumph of the enclosure movement there.

Because the process of enclosure is far advanced in the United States today, these issues are of more than historic interest. Despite the continuing erosion of our farm population, farming remains the single most important facet of the American economy. In 1985, U.S. agriculture and directly related food industries employed over twenty-two million people, more than the steel and automobile industries combined. Farming still accounts for 20 percent of the U.S. gross national product and remains the country's most valuable trade item. Ironically, as the number of people directly involved in American agriculture declined, the number of people dependent on American agriculture—both here and abroad—has skyrocketed.

This is why farming affects everyone in the country, and why it matters that many American farmers cannot make a living, even if they have good land, are willing to work until midnight, and are more or less moral people. Indeed, the saddest thing about the Lone Tree tragedy is that everyone involved was a good person: Emily Burr, who instructed Lone Tree girls in the mysteries of sweet and sour pork; John Hughes, who gave more time to philanthropy in a month than most people do in a year; and Rich Goody, who spent the last Saturday night of his life in church because he was afraid of bad weather on Sunday. Even Dale Burr, a man who murdered three innocent people in cold blood, was not without his virtues.

Dale might have been parochial in his experience—and he might have made mistakes managing the family farm—but he was not a kook and he was not stupid. He had fatal faults that were revealed under pressure like the tragic flaws of a character in a Greek play. But neighbors still recall he had his big laugh to the end. Perhaps the reason the tragedy struck people in Johnson County so hard was that they could see aspects of themselves in Dale, both good and bad.

The deeper personal tragedy of Dale Burr was the fact that he became a victim of a historic process that he himself advanced. He met the fate of his fathers face to face, and did not know it.

EPILOGUE

The early months of 1986 brought no relief for the Burrs. In January, Leslie Parizek began legal action to reclaim his farm from John Burr. In February, the Columbus Junction Bank filed a petition to foreclose the land Dale had mortgaged for the loan to buy the Parizek place. Then in early March, Leslie Parizek and his attorney, Jay Honohan, filed another suit to evict John Burr and the people to whom he had rented the Parizek house.

The Burrs' relations with the Hills Bank, which still held the mortgage on Dale Burr's home place, were understandably tenser than ever. This situation was complicated in March by another unexpected and tragic death. Bank vice-president Jim Gordon, thirty-eight, who had shouldered much of the burden after the murder of John Hughes, died suddenly of a heart attack while watching the University of Iowa Hawkeyes basketball team play in an NCAA tournament on TV. "Job stress is what got him," said Gordon's brother John, a hog buyer in Cherokee, Iowa.

"It was that plus . . . well, I don't want to talk about that."

Marilyn Goody held an auction a couple of weeks later to sell off all of Rich's farm equipment. More than three hundred people, mostly farmers in coveralls and feed hats, showed up on a sunny day in late March to look over Rich's stuff. "I don't think some of this equipment saw any rain until they pulled the equipment out for this sale," said Bob Jensen, a neighbor across the field. The auctioneer started with the smallest hand tools and worked his way up to the tractors and combine. Marilyn Goody watched most of the auction with Father Hitch. She wore a stocking cap and big square sunglasses, and never appeared to smile as people bought every single implement put up for sale, mostly at good prices.

John Burr also got some help with his debts from a State of Iowa interest buy-down program, but his legal difficulties continued to mount. In the summer of 1986, the Goody family brought a wrongful death suit against Dale Burr's estate, asking for $3 million. John Burr soon filed a nearly identical claim against his father's estate on behalf of his mother's estate, also asking for $3 million. While lawyers were impressed with this legal tactic, many people just shook their heads over the fact that the Burrs were now suing themselves. When I spoke with her in April 1986, Sheila Ross, John Burr's sister, told me: "The tragedy is still ongoing for me."

Two years later, Karen Hughes had difficulty discussing the subject in an even voice. She still lived in the dramatic cantilevered house overlooking a park in the affluent University Heights section of Iowa City. She and her daughters were well taken care of materially in the wake of the murders (John Hughes left a multimillion-dollar estate that included ten life insurance policies), but that has not helped the emotional wounds to heal. Friends say that Karen Hughes did not bring a wrongful-death suit against the Burr estate because she did not need the money, and she did not want to diminish any judgment the Goodys might be able to win on that front.

People wondered what John Burr would do, and he had a ready answer. "I'm going to farm it all," he said regarding the family holdings in the spring of 1986. Others were not convinced. "He's going to lose it all," said Johnson County Attorney Pat White, who would have prosecuted Dale Burr for murder if he had been captured alive. A strong believer in restitution for crime victims, White said he believed the $500,000 left in the Burr estate should go to the Goody and Hughes families. "A county attorney can't institute action in a case like this," he said, "but I'm going to do everything in my power to assist the Goodys in taking possession of Dale Burr's net worth."

One of the first things that John Burr did was to sell many of Dale's horses, but none of them brought more than four hundred dollars, a surprisingly low price. One person who attended the auction said the horses looked terrible, with untrimmed hooves, uncombed tails, and uncertain papers. People began to remark that John Burr himself was looking poorly. They said he seemed pallid and tentative, and did not appear to be carrying enough weight for his frame. Several said they would offer to give John a hand, but they got the feeling he did not want any help. Then in late spring John was struck with what appeared to be a stroke. Hospitalized briefly, he returned to the farm even further behind than in Dale's days.

Epilogue

On June 6, when the corn was already ankle high on most farmers' fields, he still had not planted a crop. Keith Forbes and his sons helped with part of the land, though, and John decided to plant sorghum, an unconventional but quick-growing crop in Johnson County. That summer John Burr gave two hogs to the Our Redeemer Lutheran Church's pancake and sausage breakfast. When asked if he really wanted to do that considering his financial difficulties, he replied, "With hogs worth as little as they are now, I might as well give them away." Soon, though, the price of hogs went up to near-record levels. John Burr's sorghum did well too, and it began to look as if he might be able to turn the corner.

In fact, the legal battles had hardly begun. In July 1986, the IMT Insurance Company went to court to avoid paying out on its comprehensive liability policy with Dale. IMT contended that Dale's actions on December 9 were not covered since the policy had a clause excluding "bodily injury or property damage caused intentionally by . . . the insured." Soon Dale's victims went to court to get the insurance company to post a $2.25-million bond, and both sides settled in for a lengthy legal struggle that turned on the question of whether Dale was sane at the time he committed the murders.

If Dale was legally insane when he went on his rampage, his actions could not be construed as "intentional." Then the insurance company would be required not only to pay out damages, but also to defend Dale's estate against other legal claims. John and Julia Burr, in their capacity as executors of Dale and Emily's estates, both argued that Dale was "non compos mentis." In a rare show of agreement, the Goodys' and Hugheses' attorneys concurred.

Epilogue

City Attorney Pat White was one who did not agree, despite his desire to see restitution for the victims. "Dale was in a rage clearly," he said, "but that is different from insanity. His actions were far too calculated for that." As the IMT suit dragged on, the Burrs continued to lose property. The next to go was the Siever place, which the Hills Bank took in exchange for a several-hundred-thousand-dollar reduction in the Burrs' debt.

In 1989, John Burr was still farming several hundred acres of the Burr land, and still living alone in the old home place where he was raised. Marilyn, Rachel, and Mark Goody likewise remained on their farm nearby, although Marilyn had gone back to work in Iowa City. The Goody land was plowed and planted every year, but Rich's hog houses stood empty and almost surgically clean.

Meanwhile, John Burr's hog operation was going strong. I remember talking to him one afternoon after hog chores in the fall of 1986. A little late, he came flying up the drive in Dale's battered old pickup truck, which he still used for work. He was wearing a red Firestone baseball hat and a yellow Yoder Feed T-shirt.

Although obviously tired from a long day, he was pleasant and soft-spoken. The only time there was a flash of iron in his voice was when he talked about his plans for the future. "I've made up my mind I'm going to go on farming right here," he said, "even if it's only hogs on five acres."

When I asked him how the hunting was that fall, he said he had given up pheasant hunting. "I just look now," he said, gazing out across the fields toward the blue Lone Tree water tower and his parents' still unmarked graves.

ACKNOWLEDGMENTS

I want to express my gratitude to the many residents of Johnson County, Iowa, who shared their thoughts and memories with me. I also owe a substantial debt to the scores of journalists from all over the country who covered the tragic events of December 9, 1985. Most of all, though, I want to thank my friend and editor, Barbara Grossman, who called one rainy afternoon and asked if I wanted to write a book on the American farm crisis keyed to Dale Burr's rampage.

INDEX

215

Index

Index

217

Index

Index

Index